SECURING A PLACE FOR
READING IN COMPOSITION

SECURING A PLACE FOR READING IN COMPOSITION

The Importance of Teaching for Transfer

ELLEN C. CARILLO

UTAH STATE UNIVERSITY PRESS
Logan

Published by Utah State University Press
An imprint of University Press of Colorado
5589 Arapahoe Avenue, Suite 206C
Boulder, Colorado 80303

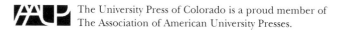 The University Press of Colorado is a proud member of
The Association of American University Presses.

The University Press of Colorado is a cooperative publishing enterprise sup-
ported, in part, by Adams State University, Colorado State University, Fort
Lewis College, Metropolitan State University of Denver, Regis University,
University of Colorado, University of Northern Colorado, Utah State
University, and Western State Colorado University.

The paper used in this publication meets the minimum requirements of the
American National Standard for Information Sciences—Permanence of Paper
for Printed Library Materials. ANSI Z39.48–1992

ISBN: 978-0-87421-959-3 (paper)
ISBN: 978-0-87421-960-9 (ebook)

Library of Congress Cataloging-in-Publication Data
Carillo, Ellen C.
  Securing a place for reading in composition : the importance of teaching for
transfer / Ellen C. Carillo.
     pages cm
     ISBN 978-0-87421-959-3 (paperback) — ISBN 978-0-87421-960-9 (ebook)
1. Composition (Language arts). 2. Reading. 3. English language—
Rhetoric—Study and teaching. I. Title.
  LB1575.8.C37 2014
  372.47—dc23
                         2014017560

Cover illustration © Artex67/Shutterstock

CONTENTS

ACKNOWLEDGMENTS

I must begin by extending my deepest gratitude to my editor at Utah State University Press, Michael Spooner, for believing in this project from the start. I appreciate his patience and encouragement through the long review and revision process and the risk he took accepting a manuscript on a topic that was not on the field's radar when I proposed it several years ago.

For their pointed and detailed feedback on my work, I am grateful to the anonymous reviewers at Utah State University Press and appreciate how carefully Laura Furney, Beth Anderson, Kelly Lenkevich, Karli Fish, and Daniel Pratt prepared this manuscript. Thank you to my colleagues at UConn, including Tom Deans, Lynn Bloom, and Tom Recchio who offered insightful comments and suggestions at various stages of this project. This book is significantly better for all of this feedback.

Many others have helped me complete this manuscript through collaborations on conference panels, conversations about reading and writing, and simply through their friendship and unwavering encouragement: Kirstin Collins Hanley, Michael Bunn, Mariolina Salvatori, Patricia Donahue, the members of The Role of Reading in Composition Studies Special Interest Group, as well as my fellow Writing Coordinators at UConn and my colleagues in English and Freshman English at UConn, Waterbury.

I would also like to thank those who participated in the study detailed in this book. I appreciate the time these instructors and students spent with me discussing how they experience the relationship between reading and writing in their classes. I was struck by their willingness to offer me the little free time they had—and sometimes free time they had to make—in order to participate. For some this meant answering my questions while simultaneously placating rambunctious toddlers or crying babies in the background or speaking with me in the car while driving from one teaching job to another. For others it meant taking time away from the Conference on College Composition and Communication convention in St. Louis for the interviews I conducted at a nearby coffee shop. I must also thank the Conference on College Composition and Communication for supporting this study with a Research Initiative Grant, as well as the University of Connecticut's Research Fund for their material support that helped make this book possible.

With this book's emphasis on teaching, I would be remiss not to thank the fine teachers I was fortunate to encounter over the years, including those at Muhlenberg College and the University of Pittsburgh. The former saw promise in my work and encouraged me to continue onto graduate school and the latter helped me to see the importance of teaching reading alongside writing. I was thoroughly shocked when I left Pitt and realized this practice is not a given within the field. Perhaps one day it will be.

Thank you to my parents, Beverly and Joseph Gerber, and my sister Betsy for their ongoing support even though the path I chose was so unfamiliar to our family. And finally, thank you to my husband Dave, without whom I could not have finished this book. He often played both mom and dad to our boys especially during the summer so that I could focus exclusively on writing. My work is considerably better for his consistent guidance and thoughtful feedback. And a special thanks to my two boys, Avi and Harris, both born during the course of writing this manuscript, for being great nappers, and thus affording me the time I needed to complete this project.

SECURING A PLACE FOR
READING IN COMPOSITION

1

INTRODUCTION

In the final months of 2009, the WPA listserv (WPA-L) saw an onslaught of detailed responses to an initial post with the deceptively simple subject line: "How well do your students read . . . ?" The complete question, posted in the body of the email, sent to the listerv on October 27 by Bob Schwegler (2009) from the University of Rhode Island read: "How well do your students read complex texts—other than literary texts?" With more than fifty responses in just a few days, it became clear that this was an issue that interested a range of subscribers, many of whom responded to the question by drawing on their classroom teaching practices. Some listed useful assignments and methods (e.g., rhetorical analyses, annotation) while others wrote about textbooks that encourage the teaching of reading in composition such as Bartholomae and Petrosky's *Ways of Reading* and Rosenwasser and Stephen's *Writing Analytically.*

The majority of the respondents, however, went outside of composition to think about reading. Some encouraged those in composition to turn to the Education Departments at their schools. Others such as Jennifer Wells (2009) shared websites for high school English teachers and names of speakers and other scholars (e.g., Frank Smith) working within K–12 whose work might be adapted for use by post-secondary instructors. Arguing, on the other hand, that literature instructors are especially well-equipped to teach reading, Ryan Skinnell (2009) looked to the New Critics as exemplars of literature instructors committed to the teaching of reading, which he defines as "comprehension, close reading, critical assessment. I will not, can not, shall not claim that literature specialists are the best reading teachers in the world," writes Skinnell, "But

DOI: 10.7330/9780874219609.c001

I will, can, and shall claim that they are expert readers with the potential for teaching reading as a valuable function of what English departments claim to do." Overall, the posts are best characterized by Patricia Donahue's (2009) post wherein she writes: "It is curious to me that when the subject of reading comes up those of us in rhetoric/composition veer in one of two directions: towards literature, saying that's what those people teach; or towards developmental reading specialists, trained in more qualitative methods. But we don't refer to the substantial body of work done on reading in our own field (especially in the late eighties to early nineties)—particularly on the interrelationship of reading and writing. Why not?" Interestingly, although subscribers continued to respond to this thread for days after Donahue posted her provocative question, no one addressed or answered it except Bill Thelin (2009b) who suggested "an online study/reading group to discuss the research Patricia talks about" in order to "help us implement it and perhaps contribute to the body of knowledge by creating new applications."

WPA-L subscribers are not the only ones in the field for whom the 1980s and 1990s is not a reference point for scholarship on reading. Histories of the field such as Stephen North's *The Making of Knowledge in Composition* do not include a discussion of those scholars within composition for whom reading pedagogy was as important as writing pedagogy. More recently, Susan Miller's 1,760-page *The Norton Book of Composition Studies* and Villanueva and Arola's (2011) 899-page *Cross-Talk in Comp Theory: A Reader*, two anthologies that are often used in graduate courses in rhetoric and composition, neglect to include essays on reading despite the overwhelming presence of these in the field during the 1980s and 1990s. This moment wherein attention to reading flourished within composition is simply not a part of standard accounts of composition's history. Neither is it represented in texts used to educate scholars new to the field. Why didn't the subject of reading become integral to how composition defined itself as a field since compositionists were studying reading and developing reading pedagogies at this disciplinary-defining moment? Over the years, hypotheses have been offered as to why reading did not establish itself as one of the field's primary subjects. The first holds the "great divorce" (also called the "great divide") responsible, noting that as composition worked hard to define itself against literary studies in the 1980s it held especially tight to writing instruction since that was the one element that separated these fields from each other. Related to this first hypothesis is the theory that a struggle over disciplinary identity may have been the cause, a struggle that was marked by composition's investment in separating itself not only from literary theory, but also from reading instruction as it was defined by education (particularly K–12). Another hypothesis is that reading as a *subject* of inquiry has not disappeared, but that the term "reading" has been subsumed by the broader term "literacy" in much the same way Paul Butler found that attention to style never disappeared from composition, but simply migrated to other areas within composition, including genre studies among others. A final hypothesis has to do with the "social turn," wherein the field's attention turned toward writing's social dimensions and situated the writer as a social being affected by cultural, political, and social forces. While these are viable hypotheses, I am not convinced that they tell the entire story.

Each of these hypotheses looks *outside* of what I will call "the reading movement"[1] in order to account for reading's inability to take hold in the field. And, while Chapter 4 details the aspects of the discussions from the 1980s and early 1990s that are worth recovering, this book also contends that one contributing factor may actually lie *within* the scholarship from that movement. This project recovers that scholarship to explore precisely how scholars articulated their theories of reading and how the conflation of the terms "reading" and "literature," as well as differing goals of the scholars, were obstacles that prevented reading from securing its place as a primary focus of the field. These dissonances reigned, and as Kathleen McCormick (1994, 5) points out, in the "absence of such dialogue, work in reading remains fragmented and its transformative capacities limited."

Looking closely at the proliferation of scholarship on reading from the 1980s and 1990s both to imagine what went wrong, as well as to describe what seems recoverable and useful from that moment, this book considers what might be involved in reanimating discussions about reading within composition. Studying this moment provides access to how it was that these scholars managed to redefine reading instruction as something other than remedial and expand the intellectual and pedagogical sphere of rhetoric and composition—even for just a short period—to include theories and pedagogies of reading.

As I make the final edits on this introductory chapter, initially drafted a few years ago, I am excited to point out that we may again be entering a period like the 1980s and 1990s wherein compositionists are starting to (re)turn to questions surrounding the teaching of reading in composition. As Salvatori and Donahue (2012) note in their most recent *College English* piece, "Stories about Reading: Appearance, Disappearance, Morphing, and Revival," there seems to be a revival of interest in reading in the field of composition. I imagine this book contributing to this revival by offering an account of reading's demise, some historical antecedents that may help explain it, as well as some recommendations for reintroducing discussions of reading. Taking into consideration how and why, historically, reading has been neglected by composition and pairing that history with a current, qualitative study of the place of reading in contemporary first-year composition classrooms (Chapter 2) allows me to make recommendations for effectively reanimating discussions of reading in composition and productively integrating attention to reading into first-year composition classrooms.

READING AND WRITING: COUNTERPARTS IN THE CONSTRUCTION OF MEANING

The term "reading" throughout this book is not simply referring to the scanning of words on a page. Although the term "composition" has, for years, been used synonymously with the term "writing" in curricula and scholarship, this study—like the scholarship from the 1980s and 1990s—is founded on the idea that both practices of reading and writing involve the construction—or *composition*—of meaning. In defining reading as an active enterprise, this study follows the lead of Ann E. Berthoff, David Bartholomae, Anthony Petrosky, Alice Horning, Mariolina Salvatori, Patricia Donahue, Donna Qualley, Linda Flower, and James R. Squire, among others, whose scholarship and teaching locate reading and writing as forms of inquiry and ways of making meaning. Berthoff (1982) has argued that "at the heart of both reading and writing is interpretation, which is a matter of seeing what goes with what, how this goes with that. Interpretation," she writes, "has survival value. We and all of our fellow creatures must interpret in order to stay alive. The difference between them and us is language: It is language that enables us to go beyond interpreting to interpret our interpretations. This spiraling circularity empowers all the activities of mind involved in meaning making" (85). Squire (1983, 581) sees reading and writing as two operations that "actively engag[e] the learner in constructing meaning, in developing ideas, in relating ideas, in expressing ideas." Bartholomae and Petrosky (1986, 14) locate reading as an activity that "centers itself on a general inquiry into the possible relations between a reader and a text, something that can be represented by studying the specific written responses of specific readers." In "From Story to Essay: Reading and Writing," Petrosky (1982, 20) describes reading in terms of understanding: "Reading, responding, and composing are aspects of understanding, and theories that attempt to account for them outside of their interactions with each other run the serious risk of building reductive models of human understanding." Qualley's (1997) "essayistic reading" also assumes that reading is a form of inquiry that is transactional in nature, but she argues that her approach has a wider application in that it may be used by students and teachers alike and offers a "both/and" stance that she believes is lacking in Bartholomae and Petrosky's method. A "form of hermeneutic inquiry into texts," Qualley's approach "is not a way of reading (or writing) that many students have experienced. . . . In essayistic reading and writing, readers and writers put themselves at risk by opening themselves to multiple and contrasting perspectives of others. At the same time, however, they reflexively monitor their own beliefs and reactions to the process," since "readers need to be both the subject and object of their reading (they read themselves as they read the text)." This "ensures that their encounter with ideas will be dialogic and bidirectional rather than unidirectional" (62).

None of these scholars defines reading and writing as mechanical or instrumental processes. Instead, they highlight the hermeneutical nature of reading and writing (some, drawing directly from Wolfgang Iser and Hans-Georg Gadamer) and how these practices can be used to foster understanding and self-reflexivity. Adopting this formulation, this study also posits that reading is a deliberate intellectual practice that helps us make sense of—interpret—that which surrounds us. And, that which surrounds us includes so much more than published texts. We also read our own writing, our own and others' belief systems, as well as everything from ideological and social structures to political and advertising campaigns to each other's expressions and our personal interactions. The range of activities that falls under what might be called "reading" demands a more complex practice than a one-size-fits-all mechanical process of decoding. The emphasis that the scholars writing in the 1980s and 1990s place on self-reflexivity and (meta)cognition acknowledges the complexity of reading and its many manifestations, and, thus, becomes crucial to my recommendations for renewing discussions about reading in composition.

READING IN COMPOSITION: THE LAST TWO DECADES

Prior to a 2012 change in the Conference on College Composition and Communication's (CCCC) call for proposals, it had been almost two decades since composition's professional organization encouraged panels and presentations on reading. Salvatori and Donahue (2012, 210) found that although in the 1980s several subject clusters on the CCCC's call for proposals invited panels and presentations about reading or reading-writing connections, more recently and for roughly "seventeen years the word 'reading' was completely invisible.'" Others have conducted similar studies: David Jolliffe (2003, 128) notes that the word "reading" only appeared in the titles of two sessions at the 2003 CCCC's meeting where there were 574 concurrent sessions, special interest groups, and workshops. Moreover, Debrah Huffman (2007, 5) found that "combined, the number of sessions and individual presentations devoted to either reading or analytical reading comprises scarcely one percent of the total presentations in any given year."

Certainly, tracing the presence of the word "reading" in the CCCC's call for proposals does not outright prove anything. But, these studies suggest, along with the range of other evidence I offer in this introductory chapter and beyond, that reading has seemingly disappeared from composition's disciplinary landscape. It is worth noting that Salvatori and Donahue (2012) offer an alternate hypothesis—namely that reading is omnipresent in composition, "suffusing" all that we do in the discipline, and is thus taken for granted and unexplored. Despite our differing perspectives, though, our conclusions remain the same: To neglect reading altogether (my position) or "reduce reading to a kind of pervasive background influence and to push it to the borderlines" (211) is problematic because composition loses the opportunity to increase its knowledge about writing's counterpart in the construction of meaning and to imagine the implications of this knowledge for the teaching of writing.

For the most part, discussions of reading as it relates to composition focus on *which* texts one should teach in the composition classroom (if any at all) rather than the practice of reading itself. In other words, composition scholars spend time focusing on reading(s) as a noun—rather than on reading as a verb, as a practice or process. For example, in what has come to be called the Lindemann-Tate debate, compositionists Erika Lindemann and Gary Tate discussed the role of literature in first-year composition courses. In the pages of *College English*, Lindemann

(1993) details her position that literature should not be taught in first-year composition because literary texts don't adequately represent the type of writing students will be expected to complete in the academy. Still, she notes that the course should pay attention to reading. In fact, she insists that paying attention to reading is an integral part of first-year composition, noting that "we need to join students in exploring these sites of composing" (316). Tate and others who entered the discussion, however, conflated the teaching of reading with the teaching of literature without recognizing the distinction upon which Lindemann's argument depends. Tate (1993), for example, focuses exclusively on text selection noting that "we should not deny our students the pleasure and profit of reading literature" (319) since this "excellent writing" helps students improve as writers, a point he does not develop except to say that his vision "excludes no texts" (321) in the composition classroom.

More recently, in *Profession 2009,* which focuses on "The Way We Teach Now," many scholars address the status of reading within English studies. While David Steiner's (2009) "Reading" and Mark Edmundson's (2009) "Against Readings" take the usual approach to discussing reading as a noun rather than a verb, Gerald Graff (2009) approaches the issue differently, contending that it matters more *how* we read than what we read in "Why How We Read Trumps What We Read." Still, this focus on the very process of reading compels him to explore an implication of his argument that ultimately has more to do with the substance of the readings (noun) rather than the process the title suggests he may pursue. He admits that his argument may seem to lead to the following "untenable conclusion": "If how we read trumps what we read, if any text can be made hard by the way students are asked to read and talk about it, then it would seem to follow logically that it makes no difference which texts a teacher assigns. A syllabus consisting entirely of texts on the *Vanna Speaks* level (or of nothing but comic books or VCR programming manuals) could presumably be as intellectually challenging and possess as much educational value as a syllabus consisting of established classics" (72). The remainder of Graff's essay explores this implication until he arrives at the conclusion that "the kinds of texts we assign do matter" (73), thereby shifting his focus from the process of reading to what *types* of readings to teach.

Until about a year ago when we began to see a smattering of articles attending to reading-writing connections, the most consistent scholarship on reading came not from composition, but from education, and it rarely addresses the post-secondary level. The 2009 edition of *Open Words: Access and English Studies*, a journal dedicated to post-secondary teaching, challenges this trend and offers a model of collaboration across disciplinary boundaries. The journal focuses on "political, professional, and pedagogical issues related to teaching composition, reading, creative writing, ESL, and literature to open admissions and non-mainstream student populations." Editor William Thelin describes the special issue as one that explores the ways in which reading research from K–12 educators and educational theorists can and should inform college-level teaching, and describes his own need to "strengthen [his] relationship with ideas drawn from K–12 educators, educational theorists, and researchers in both secondary and post-secondary institutions" (Thelin 2009a, 3). "If reading matters—and most of us think it does," writes Thelin, "we have to teach students how to do it . . . we all must become reading teachers" (4). It is that very idea—that we must all become reading teachers— that is partially responsible for post-secondary instructors' choice not to teach reading in their classrooms, despite their overwhelming sense that students need help in this area. For *professors* to teach reading would be to "lower" themselves to do work that should have been done by K–12 *teachers*. Yet, as Kathleen McCormick (1994) points out, plenty of literature instructors are already teaching reading, but refuse to identify themselves as doing so: "Many literary theorists who specifically teach students new reading practices, and who ask students to read from particular perspectives with new sets of concerns—from perspectives of gender, race, or cultural politics, for instance—do not represent themselves as teachers of reading, and consequently miss an important opportunity both to locate the practices they are encouraging within students' own educational reading history and to develop connections with others in the field who may share many of their goals" (McCormick 1994, 6).

Because to teach reading is considered remedial work by many in English studies, the teaching that they do does not strike them as reading instruction at all. Certainly students do know how to read—as in decode language—when they get to college, but most are not prepared to deliberately engage in sophisticated forms of reading that are defined by inquiry. Jeanne Henry (2009, 64) has described this issue as follows: "My freshmen were very much *able* to read; they were simply disinclined *to* read. As a result, they lacked experience with different genres, writing styles, and degrees of difficulty." Not everyone in English studies—or in composition for that matter—is willing to recognize the nuances that Henry does, and are quick, instead, as McCormick points out, to describe reading instruction as remedial and relevant to K–12 *teachers* rather than postsecondary English *professors*. I experienced this first-hand when looking for a publisher for this manuscript. Reviewers and the editor at a well-known composition publishing house concluded that this project was not relevant to their book series in composition. One reviewer wrote: "Since most of reading research is done at K–12 and [our] series usually publishes about adult writing, I'm wondering how that fits into the project." The other reviewer agreed, "If students reaching us in college cannot 'read' as in decipher writing, then maybe they shouldn't be there." The series editor concurred with these comments and suggested that Columbia Teachers College Press, which publishes scholarship almost exclusively relevant to K–12, "might be a good fit." Not only do both reviewers and the editor reify the false binary opposition between reading and writing, locating the former in K–12 research and pedagogy, but the second reviewer also oversimplifies what it means to read, noting that "if students reaching us in college cannot 'read' as in decipher writing, then maybe they shouldn't be there." While I wouldn't go so far as to say these are representative responses to this project, unfortunately they are not rare, either. Ultimately, they underscore the uphill battle of reanimating discussions about reading in composition.

Of course, this book is not about teaching students how to "decipher writing," but rather about the importance of opening up discussions, once again, about reading's connection to writing and how composition as a field can enrich its research and scholarship in this area and, ultimately, better support the teaching of writing. Despite the complexity of the act of reading itself, as suggested by compositionists' research on reading that emerged in the 1980s and 1990s, attending to reading often continues to be framed as remedial work. If we continue to allow reading instruction to be defined in this way, then there will continue to be a lack of interest in pursuing the subject. Composition instructors will be deprived of resources for teaching and the field as a whole will be deprived of new knowledge that might be developed from reading research conducted within the context of methods of composing.

Reanimating discussions about reading might mean synthesizing (1) what we know about composition's historically vexed relationship to reading, (2) the problems, as well as the potential that characterize the wealth of scholarship on reading from the 1980s and 1990s, and (3) any information we might be able to cull about the current place of reading in first-year composition courses. This book takes on that challenge.

THE IMPORTANCE AND URGENCY OF THIS WORK

To leave the work of defining reading to other fields, even related fields like literary studies and education, means that composition is forfeiting the right to define reading and its relationship to writing. Related to this is the urgency of this work for the teaching of first-year composition. Since the majority of scholarship on reading is almost 20 years old, instructors are at a loss for current research and scholarship to support their teaching of writing. David Jolliffe (2007, 478) has noted the problems this poses: "Because the topic of reading lies outside the critical discourse of composition studies, these instructors would not have access to ample resources to help them think about a model of active constructive reading in their courses or about strategies for putting that model into play." Adler-Kassner and Estrem (2007, 36) explain similarly that "at the same time as instructors ask for more explicit guidance with reading pedagogy, that pedagogy is rarely included in composition research, graduate composition course, or first-year writing programs' developmental materials." Abandoning reading as a subject worthy of sustained attention and research in the field puts composition instructors in an untenable position wherein, although reading undeniably plays some role in first-year composition, these instructors lack the resources to develop reading pedagogies that will complement their writing pedagogies. The first-year composition instructors I interviewed as part of a qualitative study, detailed in Chapter 2, regularly described their commitment to, but also their discomfort attending to reading in the classroom. These instructors largely believe that they lack the training and the theoretical framework to teach reading effectively. Without professional discourse that addresses the role that reading might play in the field broadly, and in the first-year composition classroom, specifically, instructors do not have the tools necessary to support the development of reading pedagogies that would allow for more comprehensive literacy instruction in first-year composition.

Once we know more about reading, we can take steps to revise the mission and outcomes statements important to our field, including the Writing Program Administrators (WPA) Outcomes Statement for First-Year Composition[2] and the Conference on College Composition and Communication (CCCC) Position Statements and Resolutions. Reopening discussions about reading has the potential to help organizations like WPA and CCCC articulate more concretely what they mean by "critical reading" when they list it as one of the elements of first-year composition instruction. Without defining this term and elaborating on how the course's reading is connected to its writing these statements remain incomplete. This book aims to provide a contemporary view of reading's place in first-year composition, as well as some history, both of which are potentially useful in revising these statements.

I should note that the connections this study draws between reading and writing are not supported unequivocally within the field. Sharon Crowley (1998, 13) asserts that "the act of composing differs appreciably from the act of reading." Crowley sees the humanist approach to the first-year composition course as detrimental because modern humanists privilege reading over writing. "The point of a humanist education, after all," writes Crowley, "is to become acquainted with the body of canonical texts that humanists envision as a repository of superior intellectual products of Western culture." A second problem that Crowley notes is that "humanism takes a respectful attitude toward already-completed texts, while composition is interested in texts currently in development as well as those that are yet to be written" (13). While Crowley is moving between first-year composition and the field of composition as a whole, she seems to say that to include reading in composition would be to undermine the teaching of writing since reading is always necessarily privileged.[3] Crowley, however, is inconsistent in how she uses the very term "reading." Initially, she is concerned with the "*act* of reading," reading as a process or practice, but quickly moves to discuss reading as a noun as she describes humanism's "respectful attitude toward already-completed texts." In so doing, she shifts the conversation from one about the relationship between the "act of composing" and the "act of reading" to one about the content and value of the texts themselves. Her argument offers an example of this fairly common, but often unrecognized move in discussions about reading in composition. Moreover, it raises questions about why composition has consistently rejected reading. If, for example, composition has historically embraced literary texts as its primary documents, and reading falls within the purview of literature courses, then why hasn't reading become one aspect of the teaching of composition?

WHAT THIS BOOK DOES NOT ADDRESS

Although readers may expect a chapter on how the emergence of multi-modal and new media literacies affects discussions about reading (and writing) pedagogies, this book does not contain one. Patricia Harkin (2005) could not have anticipated the emergence of the field of new media literacies, yet she recognizes the risk this book takes by returning to earlier scholarship on (print-based) reading: "Unfortunately for those who wish to take up these challenges [by paying attention to reading in the writing classroom], the thinkers who could help us most have faded from the discussion. They taught us that accounts of reading acts need not dwindle into sets of restrictive instructions in what particular texts mean. From their work, a pedagogy is still recoverable. It might seem unlikely that a professionalized professoriate committed to the 'new' would voluntarily return to work that first appeared a quarter-century ago. To do so would require a confident professoriate, more committed to social action than to professional prominence, willing to take risks in order to teach better. Composition studies, historically, has so defined itself" (Harkin 2005, 422). As Harkin suggests, it is tempting to focus exclusively on the newly emerging areas of interest within composition rather than reconsidering subjects that may no longer seem relevant. While scholars such as Gail Hawisher, Cynthia Selfe, and Cheryl Ball, among others, are already doing important work in new media studies, some research suggests the new technologies these scholars are exploring are not quite making their way into classrooms. For example, Kathleen Blake Yancey (2004, 438) noted in her Chair's address at the CCCC convention in San Antonio that despite great technological advances particularly in the area of literacy studies, composition instructors have yet to embrace these new approaches and "many of us continue to focus on print" (438). Daniel Anderson et al. (2006, 69) investigated "what composition teachers were doing with multimodal composing" and similarly concluded that "individual teachers who specialized in digital media studies were doing the majority of this work and that these efforts did not extend to department-wide or program-wide curricula" (69). Although multimodal composition and other new media technology-based work has likely proliferated in the years since Yancey and Anderson spoke to this issue, print-based reading still plays a large role in classrooms, a point corroborated by the first-year writing instructors I spoke to during the qualitative study I detail in Chapter 2.

Moreover, the traditional elements of print-based literacy remain crucial to new literacies and will not be replaced by them. Reading scholar Donald Leu et al. (2004, 1590) and his colleagues at the University of Connecticut have described these new literacies as including "the skills, strategies, and disposition that allow us to use the Internet and other ICTs [information and communication technologies] effectively to identify important questions, locate information, critically evaluate the usefulness of that information, synthesize information to answer those questions, and then communicate the answers to others" (1590). These experts, however, are quick to point out the relationship between "foundational literacies" and emerging literacies:

> It is essential, however, to keep in mind that new literacies, such as these, almost always build on foundational literacies rather than replace them. Foundational literacies include those traditional elements of literacy that have defined almost all our previous efforts in both research and practice. These include skill sets such as phonemic awareness, word recognition, decoding knowledge, vocabulary knowledge, comprehension, inferential reasoning, the writing process, spelling, response to literature, and others required for the literacies of the book and other printed material. Foundational literacies will continue to be important within the new literacies of the Internet and other ICTs. In fact, it could be argued that they will become even more essential because reading and writing become more important in an information age. (1590–91)

This study thus proceeds on the notion that digital literacies will not replace those more foundational print-based literacies, but will necessarily inform new literacies, making these foundations that much more important. Certainly there is important work to be done, some of which is already underway,[4] on how reading on screens and electronic devices necessarily affects our reading practices, but the scope of this book prohibits the sort of in-depth attention this subject requires.

CHAPTERS

Chapter 2 establishes the exigency for this project by discussing the data collected and conclusions drawn from "Reading in the First-Year Writing Classroom: A National Survey of Classroom Practices and Students' Experiences," a qualitative study funded by a CCCC's Research Initiative Grant and conducted in the winter and spring of 2012. This qualitative study suggests the need to reanimate discussions of reading in the field because, although the writing instructors surveyed are committed to teaching reading, they are doing so—by their own admission—without adequate support or resources from their graduate training, professional development, or current research and scholarship from the field. The study consists of national surveys of first-year writing instructors and their students, as well as follow-up interviews with instructors and students. This chapter contends that focusing on first-year composition can provide insight into how the field—through the course that represents its pedagogical interests most widely in curricula—imagines the place of reading. Forty-eight percent of instructors interviewed used the term "rhetorical reading" and/or "rhetorical analysis" to describe the type of reading they teach. In the follow-up interviews, instructors spoke about how teaching rhetorical reading, and more specifically, the rhetorical reading of models, allows them to explicitly connect reading and writing in their classes. While committed to teaching these related interpretive practices simultaneously, more than half of the instructors interviewed were not secure in their abilities to teach reading. While one of their primary goals is to prepare students to read effectively beyond first-year composition, they frequently questioned the efficacy of their methods. This chapter thus argues that as the field of composition renews its commitment to thinking about reading's place in writing instruction, it becomes crucial to reanimate reading research in order to better understand how instructors can prepare their students to effectively read beyond their first year, and to provide these instructors with the means for doing so. The final chapters of this book provide these resources.

Chapter 3 seeks to offer some possible historical antecedents that may help explain how and why current first-year composition instructors have experienced the separation between reading and writing in their own graduate education and professional training. As such, the chapter provides some historical context for the rest of the book by exploring the historical separation of reading from writing in the American education system. The chapter begins by looking at the early nineteenth century at which time American colleges were still requiring instruction in rhetorical theory over the course of four years. This study of rhetoric kept reading and writing together, "a center holding together the understanding of texts and the composing of texts" (Nelson 1998, 7). By the end of the century, though, with academia's growing emphasis on specialization and the sounding of the call of the literacy crisis, writing emerged as the most important aspect of human communication. Courses such as Harvard's English A were developed to focus exclusively on the teaching of writing. The artificial separation of the different domains of literacy thus began as rhetoric gave way to courses focused on writing. In addition to this early disciplinary-defining moment, this chapter considers other moments that provide insight into the field's relationship to reading. Specifically, the chapter addresses: the rise of the New Criticism and the effect of its close reading methodology on composition; the founding of the CCCC and its professional journal *College Composition and Communication* and the presence in these venues of discussions of the place of reading in composition; the Dartmouth Seminar; and the rise of reader-response theory, an approach that foregrounds the importance of the reader in literary interpretation.

Chapter 4 explores the surge of interest in reading pedagogy that emerged in the 1980s and 1990s within composition. Specifically, the chapter considers the years 1980–1993. The year 1980 marks the publication in *College English* of English and Education scholar Charles Bazerman's groundbreaking article "A Relationship Between Reading and Writing: The Conversation Model" and 1993 marks the year of the Lindemann-Tate debate, which Marguerite Helmers (2002, 8) believes "defined the terms that were to endure: literature and writing, not reading and writing." During this time, prolific scholars from composition such as David Bartholomae, Mariolina Salvatori, Wendy Bishop, Erika Lindemann, Linda Flower, Gary Tate, Deborah Brandt, and Donna Qualley led and helped sustain discussions about the relationship between reading and writing. These scholars produced (and some continue to produce) compelling theories and research on the place of reading in composition, the connections between the two practices, and the consequences of separating these practices from one another in curricula. This chapter argues that the scholarship ultimately indicates the extent to which attention to the reading process was supplanted by attention to literature and text selection. Still, this book imagines the moment as instructive and the chapter concludes by tracing the compelling tenets that scholars introduced, crucial ideas that can productively inform how we reanimate discussions of reading in the field today.

Chapter 5 argues for reanimating these discussions by thinking about the qualitative study's conclusions in light of the scholarship from the 1980s and 1990s, as well as more recent work from the interdisciplinary field of "transfer of learning" studies. The first-year composition instructors I interviewed feel responsible for preparing their students to read effectively in other courses, but described their lack of a theoretical framework for both thinking more deeply about this and developing a reading pedagogy that would facilitate this preparation. Chapter 5 draws on scholarship from educational and cognitive psychology, as well as on research about how knowledge transfers from general education courses, in order to explore how scholars in these related fields are thinking about the issue of transfer that so many first-year composition instructors raised during their interviews.

Chapter 6 uses the research and scholarship from transfer of learning studies to argue for the adoption by composition instructors of what I call a "mindful reading" framework as a means to support students' positive transfer of reading knowledge to other courses. As the chapter explains, mindful reading is best understood as a framework within which various reading approaches fit, approaches such as rhetorical reading, close reading, and critical reading. Mindful reading is *not* another reading approach that might be added to this list. Mindful reading is, instead, a method of engagement characterized by rhetorical adaptability that supports students as they deliberate, reflect on, and practice a range of reading approaches that first-year instructors help students to cultivate. Chapter 6 also provides a brief discussion of assignments and course readings that support the teaching of mindful reading.

The epilogue summarizes the conclusions drawn from the chapters to make recommendations about how the field of composition might effectively attend to reading. It also discusses future avenues for reading research, the need to revise the field's outcome statements to better reflect the connections between reading and writing, and the importance of redesigning graduate programs in rhetoric and composition to better prepare its scholar-teachers to integrate attention to reading into writing instruction.

Appendix A consists of an annotated bibliography of citations on reading from the field of composition and English studies from roughly the last three decades. Appendix B includes materials I use in professional development workshops to support faculty's integration of attention to reading across the curriculum. Appendix C includes materials related to the qualitative study described in Chapter 2. These materials include the online survey that students and instructors completed, as well as the interview guide I used when speaking with both instructors and students who consented to follow-up interviews. Appendix C also includes a more in-depth discussion of the study's analytical methods than is presented in Chapter 2.

NOTES

1. This phrase does not do justice to the diversity of perspectives that characterize the scholarship from the period, but will need to suffice as shorthand for the corpus of scholarship produced at this time.

2. The Role of Reading in Composition Studies Special Interest Group, which I co-lead, developed and submitted suggested revisions to this statement that would address reading in more substantial and consistent ways. At press time, the recommendations were being reviewed by the WPA Outcomes Statement Taskforce.

3. For an insightful exploration of how reading (as opposed to writing) continues to be privileged in curricula see Peter Elbow's (1993) "The War Between Reading and Writing and How to End It." Elbow also offers compelling ways to create a more productive and balanced relationship between reading and writing in curricula.

4. See Daniel Keller's (2013) *Chasing Literacy: Reading and Writing in an Age of Acceleration.*

2
READING IN CONTEMPORARY FIRST-YEAR COMPOSITION CLASSES
A National Survey

As noted in the introduction, the field of composition has historically neglected the role of reading in the teaching of composition. Moreover, the one moment in the field's history—the 1980s and early 1990s wherein compositionists wrote prolifically on the subject—remains terribly underrepresented in histories of the field and its anthologies, including Susan Miller's (2009) 1760-page *The Norton Book of Composition Studies* and Villanueva and Arola's (2011) 899-page *Cross-Talk in Comp Theory: A Reader*, two anthologies that are often used in graduate courses in rhetoric and composition. Thus, graduate students rarely receive training in how to productively attend to reading in writing courses and what that attention to reading might contribute to instruction in writing.

Despite what seems to be a major oversight in graduate education in rhetoric and composition, a point to which this book will later return, contemporary first-year composition instructors largely recognize that (because reading and writing are counterparts in the construction of meaning) to leave the teaching of reading practices out of first-year composition is to offer only limited literacy instruction to their students. Yet, as this chapter details the results of a survey of first-year composition instructors, it becomes clear that the majority of these instructors do not feel as though their graduate education or professional development prepared them to effectively teach the practices of reading and writing in this way.

DOI: 10.7330/9780874219609.c002

The study I conducted, "Reading in the First-Year Writing Classroom: A National Survey of Classroom Practices and Students' Experiences," supported by the Conference on College Composition and Communication's Research Initiative Grant program, might be considered an example of RAD (replicable, aggregable, and data-supported) research, as defined by Richard Haswell, as it invites and encourages others to test and extend its findings, to potentialize what I have just begun.[1]

The "severe decline" in RAD research Haswell (2005, 215) notices in composition journals *College Composition and Communication*, *College English*, and *Research in the Teaching of English* from 1939 to 1999 leads him to argue that NCTE and CCCC are "letting others do their hard research for them," (217) which has significant implications for the field. Composition, according to Haswell, is losing its ability to "defend its central practices from outside attack" because it "lacks a coherent body of testable knowledge connected to class size, computer pedagogy, group work, part-time teaching, interdisciplinary instruction, first-year sequenced syllabi, and the list can go on" (219). Of course, to this list, I would add that composition lacks significant testable knowledge about how reading is and might most productively be taught in first-year composition courses. By leaving the subject of and research on reading instruction to other fields, such as education, composition does not capitalize on the relationship between reading and writing. This allows other fields to define reading. Refusing to engage the relationship between the two processes puts composition's credibility at stake. By neglecting writing's counterpart in the construction of meaning, composition remains vulnerable to attacks on the very notion that writing is an exercise in composing meaning as opposed to merely a transcription of thought or meaning. Taken to the extreme, both writing and reading become about finding and extracting (someone else's) meaning rather than composing one's own.

RAD research can powerfully affect the future of the discipline and its position since RAD research "is a best effort inquiry into the actualities of a situation, inquiry that is explicitly enough systematicized . . . to be replicated; exactly enough circumscribed to be extended; and factually enough supported to be verified. With RAD methodology, data do not just lie there; they are potentialized. . . . The value of RAD scholarship is its capacity for growth" (201–202). While Haswell's characterization of the field's lack of sponsorship of this research may be a bit outdated, particularly in light of the related studies I describe below, his description of RAD research is crucial to this chapter. A "best effort inquiry" into the place of reading in contemporary writing instruction, the study described in this chapter is intended to inspire additional research in order to expand the field's understanding of how instructors who are currently attending to reading in their first-year writing courses[2] are doing so.

Additional research in this area is necessary for many reasons including the size of the study's sample. As suggested above and detailed below, this chapter does not claim that the small sample of instructors is representative of all instructors teaching first-year composition. As such, my interpretations of the data collected from the surveys and interviews of these instructors are best understood as necessarily contingent on this sample. Still, surveying and interviewing first-year composition instructors gave me access to how reading is currently being taught in these classes. These methods also provided insight into how ill-prepared these instructors feel as they teach reading and the degree to which they long for resources to enrich and support their pedagogies. Reviving the field's interest in reading and reading research certainly has the potential to help create these resources, as does looking back to the scholarship from the 1980s and 1990s (see Chapter 4), but we must first expose and explore how instructors are addressing reading in their courses, the goal of this chapter.

PURPOSE

This chapter, and the study described herein, seeks to supplement my discussion of the field's professional discourse on reading in Chapter 4. Tracing the development of a field through its

publications, as does Chapter 4, has a long history in composition, but as Deborah Brandt (2011, 213) reminds us, there are
limitations to this type of study: "What is less available through
this perspective is the cumulative effect that NCTE journals
have had on their readers over time—how the studies [in them]
made their way (or did not) into the thinking and practices of
NCTE members, in their roles as researchers, teachers, WPAs
and as writers. How did articles sink in? How did the scenes of
our teaching and research adjust as a result of our encounters
with journals?" Brandt's qualification above is an important one,
and one to which this chapter attends. When paired with a study
of the field's professional discourse, data collected from surveys
and interviews of first-year writing instructors, as well as from
their students, can help to create a current picture of the field
and potentially suggest the elements that need to be taken into
consideration when proposing the reintroduction of discussions
about reading. The data collected in this study suggest what is
actually happening in classrooms, something that is not necessarily reflected in the field's journals at any given time. While I
address the student-driven aspect of my study later in the chapter, below are the general guiding questions these surveys and
interviews of first-year writing instructors sought to answer[3]:

1. To what extent and how do writing instructors overtly address
   the process of reading in their classes?

2. To what extent do writing instructors perceive a need to focus
   on reading in the writing classroom?

3. What do these efforts look like both in relation to writing
   instruction and separate from it?

4. What assumptions about the connections between reading
   and writing inform instructors' approaches to the teaching of
   writing?

5. How do instructors' professional (or other) training and experience impact the degree to which they focus on reading in the
   writing classroom?

6. What classroom materials (e.g., textbooks, assignments,
   exams) support instructors' reading and writing pedagogies?

THE STUDY'S METHOD AND SAMPLE

"Reading in the First-Year Writing Classroom: A National Survey of Classroom Practices and Students' Experiences" was conducted in the winter, spring, and early summer of 2012. This qualitative study consisted of national surveys of first-year writing instructors and their students, as well as follow-up interviews with instructors and students. While there is important work to be done on the place of reading throughout the composition curriculum, this study focuses on its place in first-year composition because it is the most widely required course in the postsecondary curriculum and, thus, reaches the most students. It is, in other words, how the work of composition is represented most significantly in curricula.

Writing program administrators at institutions across the country were asked via the Writing Program Administrators' listserv (WPA-L) to invite first-year writing instructors at both two-year/community colleges and four-year colleges and universities to participate in the electronic survey. The subscribers to the listserv were also invited to participate, themselves, if they taught first-year writing. Instructors accessed the survey through an online link and were asked to provide contact information if they were willing to participate in a follow-up interview for which they would receive a small honorarium. In order to keep the sample manageable and to be able to offer honorariums for follow-up interviews to all instructors who consented, the study's limit was set at one hundred instructors. The sample takes into consideration the first one hundred respondents.

As with any study, the sample itself, how it is developed, and how it is analyzed has a major effect on the data. When it comes to self-selected sampling, as is used in this study, the sample has the potential to skew the data in certain ways. In this particular case, the decision to participate in the study might reflect an inherent bias toward the importance of teaching reading in first-year composition. I kept this bias in mind as I developed the questions I posed. I was not interested in whether those in the sample thought teaching reading in composition was valuable since the self-selection process upon which the sample depends likely indicated as much. I anticipated that if not out-right and totally committed to teaching reading in their composition classes, the instructors who completed the survey were at least making attempts to attend to reading. My prediction was correct, and because the question of whether or not participants were addressing reading was off the table, this allowed me to speak to them in more depth about their teaching practices, theoretical approaches, and professional training. Although the instructors came from a range of backgrounds and degrees of experience, this interest in reading was consistent. The following charts and discussion below give an overview of the sample.

The fields in which these respondents earned their highest degrees show a real range. Thirty-seven percent of the respondents identified themselves as holding their highest degree in rhetoric and composition, composition, or writing studies. Twenty-eight percent of those who participated in the survey self-reported holding a degree in English or literature. Seven-percent of respondents indicated that their highest degree is in education or English education. Six percent identified themselves as holding a degree in creative writing. The rest of the respondents hold their highest degree (or an additional degree) in the following areas: journalism; folklore/ethnography; teaching; applied linguistics; music; microbiology; TESOL; and American studies.

This sample certainly has its limitations. First, and perhaps foremost, it is rather small because I was limited by the number of honorariums that I could offer participants. I realize that it is risky to draw conclusions about how reading is taught in first-year composition based on such a small sample. Thus, my interpretations of the data are just that—interpretations of a limited set of data that *may* suggest larger trends. Second, while many researchers in composition use the WPA listserv to conduct research because it provides access to thousands of composition instructors, it is important to remember that the sample used in this study cannot be generalized to represent all composition instructors and their approaches to teaching. Moreover, the sample is limited to those who either subscribe to

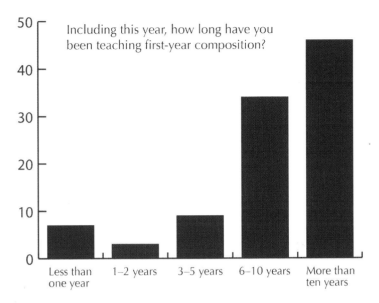

Figure 2.1. Amount of time spent teaching first-year composition

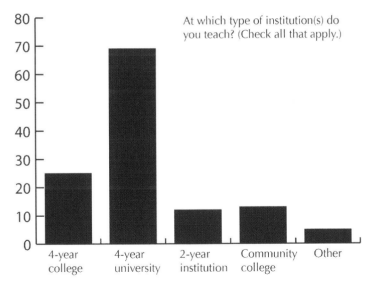

Figure 2.2. Overview of types of institutions respondents represent. Note that some instructors teach at more than one institution.

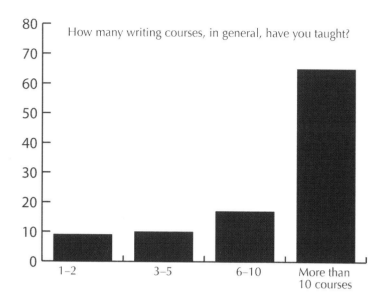

Figure 2.3. Number of writing courses respondents have taught

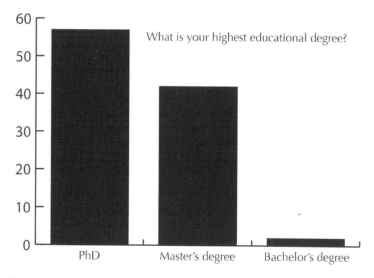

Figure 2.4. Overview of educational background of respondents

the WPA-L or teach at an institution where their WPA subscribes and chose to share the link to the online survey. Also, the nature of self-reporting, on which the surveys and follow-up interviews depend, raises its own limitations since "self-reports may blend respondents' beliefs and intentions with actual practices" (Eblen 1983, 347). While the sample cannot be understood as systematically representative of all first-year instructors' perspectives and viewpoints, it offers access to how reading currently figures into a range of first-year composition classrooms. More specifically, because of the open-ended nature of the majority of the online survey questions, this study offers insight into the terminology that is currently being used to teach reading, the goals that these instructors have set for their reading instruction, and what these instructors are drawing on from their training, background, and professional development in order to support their teaching.[4] As this chapter emphasizes, this study should be considered preliminary in nature as there is important work that might be done if one were to stratify a national sample, enlarge it, or develop it in other ways that my resources prohibited.

Each survey respondent answered every question. Out of one hundred participants, forty-three percent participated in a fifteen to thirty minute follow-up, audio-recorded interview. Instructors who became part of the survey sample due to their completion of the online survey were asked if they would be willing to share a survey link with their students. Upon completing the follow-up interviews with the instructors, I sent a link for them to share with their students if they were willing to do so. Those students who responded to the survey were asked if they would be interested in completing a follow-up, audio-recorded interview for which they would receive a small honorarium. Again, to keep the sample manageable and to be able to offer honorariums to those students who consented to follow-up interviews, the limit for the student-centered survey was set at one hundred. Ninety-three students responded to the survey. Seven and a half percent (n = 7) of these ninety-three students agreed to follow-up interviews.[5]

FINDINGS: DEFINING AND TEACHING READING

For the most part, instructors spoke about *critical reading, close reading, rhetorical reading, rhetorical analysis, reading for comprehension, analytical reading,* and *reading like a writer.* Forty-eight percent (n = 48) of instructors who completed the online survey use the term(s) "rhetorical reading" and/or "rhetorical analysis" to describe the type of reading they teach. I had not predicted this emphasis on rhetorical reading, and I am not sure many compositionists would have. As Ira James Allen's (2012) article "Reprivileging Reading: The Negotiation of Uncertainty" notes in passing, Haas and Flower's "'rhetorical reading' unfortunately never really caught on" (99). Allen's claim seems to be based on more of a hunch than data, yet prior to conducting this study I would have agreed with him. I anticipated that far more instructors would use the term "critical reading" for at least a few reasons: its terminological similarity to the ubiquitous "critical thinking"; the use of the term by the few compositionists still thinking about reading, including David Jolliffe, Alice Horning, and Nancy Morrow; and the presence of the term "critical reading" in the WPA's Outcome Statement for First-Year Composition.[6] Overall, fifteen percent (n = 15) of respondents identified themselves as teaching critical reading, making critical reading a far less common approach to teaching reading than rhetorical reading, which forty-eight percent of instructors teach. The other most common reading approaches taught within the sample are as follows: ten percent (n = 10) of the instructors I spoke to indicated that they teach "close reading"; nine percent teach reading for comprehension; three percent (n = 3) teach analytical reading; and two percent (n = 2) teach "reading like a writer." Those remaining instructors described very specific and, perhaps, idiosyncratic reading approaches such as "reading for risk," "reading for ratification," "predatory reading," and "directed skimming." It is worth noting that these "different" reading approaches likely overlap in practice even if instructors are calling them by different names.

RELATED STUDIES

My study is related to an earlier, more local study, conducted by Michael Bunn (2010), as part of his doctoral dissertation, portions of which appear in his 2013 *College Composition and Communication* article entitled "Motivation and Connection: Teaching Reading (and Writing) in the Composition Classroom." Bunn (2013) surveyed and interviewed first-year writing instructors and students at his home institution, the University of Michigan. Bunn's (2010, vi) project "compares how these instructors define and describe various reading approaches with the definitions and descriptions found in scholarship, thus offering a more complete picture of how reading is theorized and taught in first-year writing courses." While my study is not a replication of his, the survey questions I asked first-year writing instructors draw heavily on Bunn's model in order to test what happens when one poses these questions to a national audience (as opposed to instructors on a single University campus), as well as to one that is self-selected.[7]

Despite the potential in testing and extending previous studies, Davida Charney (1996, 590) points out the unfortunate lack of this type of research in composition: "It is rare for the same site or even the same kind of site to be studied by multiple scholars. Even where this should be easiest, where the sites are textual, only a few cases come to mind." Charney goes on to describe a few cases, but notes that "these scholars rarely challenge or extend each other's findings" leading her to wonder "On what basis could one decide which analyses were most productive?" Because Bunn's doctoral dissertation was comprehensive in its discussion of its context, methods, procedures, and analyses, I was able to build upon it in the ways that both Charney (and Haswell) call for.

The data collected during my study on how instructors define reading differs considerably from what Bunn found in his. Bunn (2010, 101) describes the instructors at the University of Michigan as having "incongruous definitions for reading approaches" and "confus[ing] the names of various reading approaches." Bunn notes that in many cases an "instructor is able to approximate the reading approach that he/she teaches or believes will best serve students without being able to label that approach accurately. This inability (or perhaps unwillingness) to name a reading approach is certainly reflected in the fact that of the 50 surveyed and interviewed instructors who report assigning students to read visual texts, not a single one of them names this kind of reading as visual rhetoric." Bunn recommends that instructors actually name the different reading approaches they ask their students to take since in doing so "they are passing along a distinct and measurable skill—something far more likely to motivate students to read than encouraging an unnamed approach whose benefits remain unclear" (103). My study, on the other hand, indicates that both more and less experienced instructors readily attach a name to the type of reading they taught their students. While they did not necessarily agree on the definitions of these types of reading, as is the case in the professional discourse studied in Chapter 4, they were not hesitant to name these approaches in their surveys and interviews or to call them by name in their classrooms.

Although identifying different reading approaches, the vast majority of instructors I surveyed did overtly call their students' attention to the importance of attending to reading alongside writing. Ninety-percent (n = 90) of instructors indicated that their syllabi reference the practice of reading and eighty-six percent (n = 86) noted that their syllabi actually describe reading and writing as connected practices. These instructors also consistently develop assignments that are reading-focused in order to allow students to experience the connections between reading and writing. The most common assignments described by these instructors include rhetorical analyses, informal and formal reading responses, summary writing, analyses of textual passages, annotations, and reading journal entries.

Despite their commitment to foregrounding the practice of reading in their writing courses, 51 percent of the instructors interviewed were not secure in their abilities to teach reading. Marla (2012) explained: "I would really like to know more about who our students are as readers, what they're doing as readers, how I can help them more effectively, and what that actually looks like . . . in terms of classroom design. Maybe that will just reaffirm that I've made all the right choices, but I'm pretty open to finding out that I haven't made the right choices and I should be doing something different as well. It would be really nice to see more very, very concrete and focused studies of students as readers and effective reading instruction. And as a program director, I think my instructors think that, as well."

While Marla would like to see more research into reading so she can better serve her students and the instructors she supervises, Gena (2012) registered her frustration surrounding her extensive graduate education that never focused on reading: "Not at my Master's program . . . not at my first PhD program, despite having a wonderful faculty member, and not at this . . . university that I'm at now, have I had the chance at all to talk about how college students read. It's so frustrating, and I think that I will almost have to go back, God forbid, to school to do some kind of like 'Teaching of English as a Second Language training' to really learn about how college students read." Many other instructors also felt a major gap in their academic and professional training. These instructors imagined that they might have the opportunity to think about reading in graduate programs in ESL/ELL, graduate programs in K–12 education, and professional development opportunities like the National Writing Project. In fact, Julia (2012), a graduate student earning her doctorate degree in English education and also the Writing Center Director at a four-year college described a graduate seminar she recently took and the lack of research she and her fellow graduate students were able to locate on reading at the post-secondary level: "A lot of the [research] was done on younger readers and kind of looking at what happens in the fourth or fifth grade. . . . That's where students start to lag behind in reading. . . . So there was discussion in the class on that [but] I was interested in finding as much research as I could on college readers. What I found was that there wasn't a lot . . . Our general discussion [in the class] was 'We'd love to know more.'" This sentiment— "We'd love to know more"—was repeated in various ways throughout the interviews I conducted. Because the data suggest that rhetorical reading is a widely-used approach to teaching reading in first-year composition it seems important to dwell on this approach and imagine ways of enriching the teaching of rhetorical reading, as well as other common ways of teaching reading in first-year composition.

Instructors defined rhetorical reading in ways similar to Haas and Flower in their seminal study. Haas and Flower (1988, 176) describe rhetorical readers as "concerned with constructing a rhetorical situation for the text, trying to account for author's purpose, context, and effect on the audience." They note that readers who read rhetorically build a "rich representation of text—larger than the words on the page and including both propositional content and the larger discourse context within which text function [which] is the kind of constructive reading we desire our students to do" (181). In this study, they found that experienced readers read rhetorically while less experienced readers read for content. These less-experienced readers believe that reading and writing are merely "information-exchange[s]: knowledge-telling when they write, and 'knowledge-getting' when they read" (182). As such, Haas and Flower recommend teaching rhetorical reading to undergraduate students. Despite their admission that "teaching students to read rhetorically is genuinely difficult" (182) and Richard Haswell et al.'s (1999) replication of their study "Context and Rhetorical Reading Strategies: Haas and Flower (1988) Revisited," which suggests the need to qualify Haas and Flower's findings, the contemporary composition instructors I interviewed embrace this approach to teaching reading. In these contemporary iterations of rhetorical reading, there seem to be two primary goals, to which I will return throughout this chapter:

1. To use rhetorical reading to connect the course's reading to the writing students will complete

2. To prepare students for classes beyond first-year composition

Below are representative excerpts from interviews with contemporary first-year composition instructors that speak to these goals and, in doing so, recall some of Haas and Flower's concerns surrounding content-driven reading. Erma (2012) explains that her students "are pretty good at reading for information, but not always great at reading rhetorically. . . . I try to get them in the habit of using terms of rhetorical analysis. . . . We start thinking about audience, purpose, and things like that. . . . I don't necessarily expect them to use terms of rhetorical analysis in other classes, but I think faculty in other departments would also want them to be able to say 'This is how this scientific report is working.'"

Marshall (2012) defines rhetorical analysis similarly and goes on to connect it to the writing and thinking students will do in his class:

> I'm having [my students] do rhetorical analysis. I want them to read the article and then think about the place that it's published, the audience, the purpose that the author is trying to accomplish and things like that just so they can start to see that there's structure in the writing, that there's a goal that the author is trying to get to, and that's transferable when we start talking about them writing their own papers. They can start thinking about their own purpose and the ideas they'd like to get across. . . . I'm constantly kind of grappling with the idea of reading . . . in trying to find a way to actually . . . assess these rhetorical analysis skills. . . . I don't know how well that sinks in and transfers beyond my course.

Deena (2012) also defines rhetorical reading in terms of locating a text's audience and purpose, but she expands the concept by also asking her students to consider rhetorical elements such as context, form, and genre. Reading rhetorically for these aspects of texts allows her to comment on the extent to which her students attend to the rhetorical moves they make in their own writing:

> I point out in my feedback to them. . . . this is an effective rhetorical move. I see you've done this many times. Were you aware this was a rhetorical technique? I do that to give them feedback to make them more aware of it themselves . . . I think they begin

> to get some of the basics down, at least an awareness of what they've done to appeal to their particular audience, what their purpose is, and a few other kinds of techniques they've taken into consideration . . . I can't imagine another field on campus that could really, barring communication courses, teach [students] how to read texts broadly in a rhetorical way and then actually put that into use with writing about it, which is where it all crystalizes for them.

While Deena worries that if composition courses don't teach rhetorical reading then students will have no access to this widely useful and applicable method of approaching texts, Jarna teaches rhetorical reading to combat what she calls "surface-level" reading and to prepare students for the writing they will do in her course. In order to deter students from reading simply to "get the main gist," Jarna (2012) explains: "We're looking at things like rhetorical appeal; how writers build connections with their audience; how pieces of evidence are strategically placed; what's the effect that certain introductions or conclusions have; how the visual corresponds with the text. All of this is in preparation for their own arguments that they're going to be putting together as their final project."

The instructors quoted above and others I spoke with have developed various methods to teach rhetorical reading. The most common approach is modeling in which students read in order to notice the rhetorical moves writers are making so that they can (re)produce these in their own writing. This is certainly the case for Tim (2012): "For me, it really comes down to the reason to read is for models. I try to avoid reading for content. It's a writing course, and so the work that the texts are there to do is to serve as models for the students' writing." In describing their use of models to teach rhetorical reading, some instructors also mentioned "reading like a writer," a reading strategy described and encouraged most recently by Mike Bunn (2011) in "How to Read like a Writer." This approach that teaches students to look for authors' rhetorical moves so students can replicate them in their own writing is prevalent in the excerpts above, as Marshall and Deena discuss the transferability of rhetorical techniques from students' reading into their own writing and Jarna describes reading for rhetorical moves as preparation for students' original arguments. If we believe that rhetorical reading is the most—or one of the most—common ways that reading is taught in first-year composition classrooms— it seems important to continue to dwell on how this manifests itself in the classroom as a means to better understand the extent to which this approach to reading can facilitate the two primary goals instructors shared: connecting the course's reading to its writing and preparing students for classes beyond first-year composition.

Overall, seventy-five percent (n = 36) of the forty-eight percent of instructors who teach rhetorical reading use "model," "example" or "sample" texts to do so.[8] I had not intended to focus on text selection in my study since I imagined that it might eclipse attention to reading as it often did in the scholarship from the 1980s and 1990s and continues to do so in contemporary discussions on the WPA-L. Doing so, however, proved crucial to understanding how instructors taught rhetorical reading since the texts themselves were positioned as repositories of rhetorical moves students needed to consider as they constructed their own compositions. While Bunn's (2010, 105) data was "far less conclusive" in terms of whether instructors are "simply assigning model texts in the hopes that students will recognize reading-writing connections on their own" or if they are actually teaching these, the instructors who participated in the surveys and interviews seem to be explicitly teaching students how the models should inform their own writing. Certainly instructors' descriptions of their teaching have the potential to "blend [their] beliefs and intentions with actual practices" (Eblen 1983, 347). Speaking to some of the instructors' students corroborated that these instructors are deliberately and explicitly teaching students how to apply the rhetorical moves they notice in their reading to their writing. Out of the ninety-three students who completed the survey, just over seventy-four percent (n = 69) noted that they were, in fact, motivated to read for their courses, an encouraging number particularly in light of Jolliffe and Harl's local finding that students were motivated to read outside of class but not in their first-year composition classes.

The students who agreed to participate in follow-up interviews often articulated, in detail, why they were motivated to read.[9] Sheryl (2012) described her course's readings from the textbook, *Everything's An Argument*,[10] as focused on different rhetorical strategies noting that the textbook "talked about ethos, pathos, logos, and then kind of how to structure an argument. I feel like that was helpful in structuring my own argument and kind of making sure the reasoning was all sound, the evidence was all there." Barbara (2012) experienced similar connections that motivated her to read: "Our teacher point[ed] out particular rhetorical techniques that [authors] use and encourage[ed] us to use . . . in our own writing." Wanda (2012) described how her instructor encouraged the application of sentence-level modeling of the personal narratives they read: "I found some great phrases and great sentences that I mimick[ed] and [then] created my own." Kaila described how she benefitted at both the local and global level from the way in which her instructor connected the course's reading to writing: "We read and we use[d] it as an example or as an idea to incorporate into what we wr[ote]. We read an example in our textbooks of a memoir and we['d] use it as an example of how we should write our memoir . . . [This reading also] helped me see how proper grammar is used and how sentences should be constructed. It helped me a lot with that." Although a bit skeptical about the reading for her course, Kaila (2012) said she "noticed reading, like the examples [the instructor] gave us to read . . . helped me write, so I decided that reading would help me write better." As these excerpts from the interviews suggest, motivation to read for their writing courses came from the relationship that these students were taught to see between the reading (often of models) they did and the writing expected of them. They consistently cited this as their source of motivation to read for their composition courses even if they admitted that they did not generally enjoy reading or consider themselves "readers." Although these student perspectives are consistent with Bunn's contention that overtly connecting the reading to the writing for the course motivates students, these findings complicate Jolliffe and Harl's (2008, 125) findings in which "they discovered students who were extremely engaged with their reading, but not with the reading their classes required." As such, Jolliffe and Harl recommend that composition instructors should explicitly discuss with students how "the documents that they must read relate directly to the aims and methods of learning that are most valued in the course environment, show clearly how students' reading for the course should be manifest in projects and examinations, and demonstrate specifically *how* students should read the course material" (614, emphasis in original). While neither Jolliffe and Harl's or my study claims to be conclusive, my data suggest that there are instructors who are already deliberately and explicitly doing this important work through rhetorical reading.

The instructors I spoke with teach rhetorical reading, often through the use of modeling, to help get their students reading at what they imagine is "the college level," something that forty-nine percent (n = 49) of survey respondents noted that all or most of their students are not yet doing. While none of these instructors used the term "imitation" outright, modeling has long been understood as a version of imitation, albeit one of the most flexible variations. This lends credence to Farmer and Arrington's (1993, 12) opening proclamation in their essay "Apologies and Accommodations: Imitation and the Writing Process" that "rumors of imitation's death have been greatly exaggerated" and also suggests that instructors are still hesitant to use the term "imitation" even if it describes what they are doing in their classrooms. Often, these reasons have more to do with associations imitation evokes, associations with formalism, current-traditional rhetoric, and product-driven pedagogies. If we focus on how the instructors describe their pedagogies rather than on what they call them, we see that these instructors have seemingly found ways to do what Farmer and Arrington call for in that they "engender an authentic dialogue about how imitation might be seriously rethought" (27). That instructors locate imitation or modeling within the context of rhetorical reading is perhaps nothing new as imitation—*imitatio*—is a well-documented aspect of classical rhetorical education. More significant is how these instructors conceive of modeling as the primary means to overtly and deliberately connect reading to writing in the first-year composition classroom. Audrey (2012) describes her approach as follows: "We start immediately looking at academic writing as models of discourse. . . . There's this constant going back between the text, 'What are the texts doing? What kind of models do those provide?' and then 'Okay, let's look at the prewriting you brought in through the critical lens of what we've been discussing and revise.' So there's this kind of fluent transition between the reading that they're doing and the writing that they're producing."

While Audrey (2012) seems to provide a range of models, Darla (2012) describes how she uses two particular texts in order to model a very specific "genre": "Recently I had them look at 'A Modest Proposal' . . . and then I had them read a more recent piece that I found somewhere. It's something like 'A Modest Proposal: Men Can't Drive until They're 25.' So we read the original piece first, talked about it . . . and now they're writing their own modest proposals." Darla's approach often includes "going line by line" and allowing students to ask questions as they move through Swift's text so that they can produce their own. Later chapters return to this example in more depth in order to delineate the important difference between teaching students how to analyze a genre in order to mimic its form, which is what Darla seems to be doing and "reading" the elements of that genre in order to transfer this knowledge to future contexts.

Katie (2012) does something similar to Darla, but has students in her composition and research course—the second in a two semester composition sequence—focus on understanding and modeling a text's methods. She notes, "We look at the qualitative research and quantitative research and how the journal articles that they're reading oftentimes are quantitative research [and] then how others are more like qualitative

research. Then when they write their own papers they make
some decisions about what approach they want to take, qualitative or quantitative."

Raina (2012), on the other hand, commented on the difficulty of finding appropriate published models that would work within the context of her course: "One thing I find is that a lot of textbooks, when they have these professional essays that are supposed to serve as models, it's just too different, I think, from the type of writing the students are doing, so I don't think they're effective models. . . . [I] supplement with essays written by other students so it's more what other college students have written."

Using student models—and treating them in the same way they do published texts—is, in fact, a very common approach these instructors took, unlike the instructors that Bunn (2010) interviewed at the University of Michigan who (often unintentionally) treated student texts as flawed in comparison to how they treated published texts: "Instructors at the University of Michigan repeatedly mention having students read model published texts as examples of effective writing while having students focus on locating "error" in student-produced texts" (Bunn 2010, 57). In my study, Darla described "peer workshops," which comprise fifty percent of class time, in which one or two students bring in 20 copies of their paper and students discuss these essays as modeling different rhetorical moves. Erma noted that she uses published models and student models, as well as her own writing, clarifying that she "almost always uses student writing to model things that I think they are doing well." Gena (2012) also uses a mix of student-written and published models even if they aren't perfect because she is more concerned with teaching her students how these models work: "I don't just look at professional writers and I don't just look at A+ papers. . . . I think reading articles and saying 'Okay, we like the content . . . but we totally disagree with the argument is valuable,' but I'm also saying 'What makes this work?' . . . 'How can you use that technique in your paper?'"

According to the instructors above, and many others with whom I spoke, they use both student texts and published texts to model academic discourse, methodologies, rhetorical techniques, and various other components of essays. The extensive use of modeling in first-year composition classrooms raises many avenues for future research that provide insight into ways of teaching the connections between reading and writing within the context of imitation. Such discussions are already underway thanks to the revival of stylistic studies spearheaded by Paul Butler, among others. While these discussions locate imitation within the context of style, the composition instructors who participated in my study seem interested in imitation as a bridge between the reading and writing being done in their courses. Rhetorically reading the models gives students access to the rhetorical moves writers make and imitating those moves to varying degrees allows students to practice them.

Until this point, I have considered how first-year instructors use rhetorical reading to meet their goal of connecting the practices of reading and writing. The question still remains, however, to what extent this focus on rhetorical reading meets their second goal, namely to prepare their students to read effectively in other and future classes. You will recall that Erma notes that while she does not "necessarily expect [students] to use terms of rhetorical analysis in other classes . . . [she] thinks[s] faculty in other departments would also want [students] to be able to say 'This is how this scientific report is working.'" Moreover, Marshall admits, "I'm constantly kind of grappling with the idea of reading [and] assess[ing] these rhetorical analysis skills . . . I don't know how well that sinks in and transfers beyond my course." The debate concerning whether any knowledge is truly transferrable is as old as the institution of education itself. Before considering some contemporary theories about how knowledge or learning transfers from one course or context to another—clearly a major concern of these first-year composition instructors—the following chapters look to the past in order to better understand the long-standing separation between writing and reading in the American education system; why the field of composition has largely rejected reading as a subject of inquiry; and, how contemporary composition instructors have come to find themselves ill-prepared to teach reading, writing's counterpart in the construction of meaning.

NOTES

1. Interestingly, Haswell includes a note about this new (as of 2005 when he was writing) initiative in his piece. It would be useful to consider to what extent this initiative that—by now—has awarded thousands of dollars to research-driven work in composition has impacted the amount of research and, perhaps more specifically, RAD research within the field.

2. I do not mean to conflate the field of composition with the first-year composition course as, unfortunately, too often happens. Instead, this focus on first-year composition can provide insight into how the field—through the course that represents its pedagogical interests most widely in curricula—imagines the place of reading.

3. These questions are modeled after and draw heavily on an earlier study by Michael Bunn in 2010.

4. The online survey questions and a discussion of coding methods are located in Appendix C.

5. While student participation in the online survey was strong, unfortunately, less than ten percent of these students agreed to follow-up interviews. Students' voices figure into this chapter, but because of the lack of student participation and opportunities to explain their survey answers, I focus more on the instructors' surveys and interviews. Local studies that have their institution's support and/or are being conducted by a faculty member have far more success in encouraging participation. It may be worth thinking about how national surveys can encourage a similar degree of participation so that we can begin testing and extending local, student-driven studies.

6. Although the term "critical reading" appears in this statement, it remains undefined. For more on how this statement neglects to engage with the concept of "critical reading" and "critical literacy," more generally, see Horning's (2007) "Reading across the Curriculum as the Key to Student Success."

7. Another related study was conducted by David A. Jolliffe and Alison Harl at their institution, the University of Arkansas. Like Bunn's, theirs is also an example of local, institutionally-bound research. In "Studying the 'Reading Transition' from High School to College: What Are Our Students Reading and Why?," Jolliffe and Harl (2008, 600) describe their investment in "helping [their] faculty understand salient aspects of [their] students' reading experiences and develop key strategies for developing . . . students' reading histories." They set out to discover how first-year students taking composition "perceived and effected the transition from high school to college as readers." In order to do so they "studied the reading habits and practices of twenty-one first-year composition students" by

having students self-report their reading habits and keep a reading journal for two weeks.

8. This emphasis on model texts in writing instruction emerges, as well, in some local studies, suggesting that this practice may be widespread. In addition to the prevalence of this approach in the pedagogies described by the instructors that Bunn interviewed, Bartholomae and Matway's (2010) "The Pittsburgh Study of Writing" describes instructors' use of model texts in undergraduate composition courses at their university.

9. See Appendix C for the complete student survey and the student interview guide.

10. Perhaps it is worth noting that in this textbook that draws heavily on classical rhetoric, editors Lunsford, Ruszkiewicz, and Walters (2010, viii) make a claim to transferability, noting that they have "searched for examples of research writing that use a range of methodologies, including case studies, quantitative research, and ethnography, with the goal of giving students practice for analyzing the sorts of arguments they will be assigned in their various courses." Unfortunately, transfer is characterized as something that will seemingly automatically happen simply because students practice analyzing a range of types of arguments.

3

HISTORICAL CONTEXTS

Some of the insights gleaned from the survey of first-year writing instructors, particularly those concerning their lack of teaching preparation, may leave one wondering how exactly composition—a field so invested in literacy and pedagogy—has come to largely neglect the practice of reading, which few will dispute is inextricably linked to the practice of writing and thus the teaching of writing. Tracing some historical antecedents, this chapter posits potential reasons for this contemporary situation.

This chapter begins in the nineteenth century, a time of great change as attention to reading, writing, and speaking as integrated domains of rhetoric was giving way to the prioritization of written composition over and above reading and speaking. This major shift in American education, as well as other shifts detailed below, offers an important historical context for considering the place of reading in composition. This earliest moment and the other moments this chapter studies, including the rise of the New Criticism and the effect of its close reading methodology on composition; the founding of the Conference on College Composition and Communication and its professional journal *College Composition and Communication*; the Dartmouth Seminar; and the rise of reader-response theory inform the positions that compositionists will take in the 1980s and 1990s in regard to the place of reading in the field and first-year writing classrooms. Moreover, in their anticipation of some of these very positions, this context suggests that these positions are historically grounded in assumptions that date as far back as the field of composition itself. A single chapter that considers all of these moments cannot do justice to each. As such, this chapter is best understood as a rough sketch, a necessarily incomplete history,

DOI: 10.7330/9780874219609.c003

rather than an in-depth consideration of these disciplinary-defining moments. Still, while not all-encompassing, this chapter provides insight into the historically strained relationship between composition and reading. By fostering a better understanding of composition's ambivalence toward the place of reading in writing instruction, this chapter not only contextualizes the in-depth study of the discourse on the topic that emerged in the 1980s and 1990s, but better positions composition to reintroduce these connections in deliberate and compelling ways. Although this chapter does not intend to offer a complete history of the field, it does draw on and is indebted to the important and more comprehensive work of the field's historians, including James Berlin, Sharon Crowley, Robert Connors, Susan Miller, John C. Brereton, Stephen North, and Byron Hawk.

FROM RHETORIC TO COMPOSITION

As Robert Connors (1986, 179) notes, "Rhetoric entered the nineteenth century as a discipline based around pedagogy of large lectures and accepting the idea of mental discipline . . . rhetoric exited the nineteenth century as the new discipline of composition, based around large lecture-sized discussion classes, accepting the idea of constant writing practice as central to education." Until approximately the middle of the century, American colleges were still based on the classical rhetorical model, requiring instruction in rhetorical theory over the course of students' four years. Students were also required to partake in lessons in oratory and written composition. Classical rhetoric's insistence on the links among these practices informed American college education until the middle of the nineteenth century. As is well known, this classical model largely involved students' breaking down texts into their rhetorical components in order to understand them in terms of their rhetorical effects, effects that could then be imitated in their own written compositions.

Considering the textbooks from this era offers some insight into pedagogical practices, including those surrounding reading, since at this particular moment composition had no professionals and, as Connors (1986, 178) points out, "composition theory and pedagogy were overwhelmingly shaped by one great force: textbooks." Moreover, there "was only one journal [the *English Journal*] in the field," that "as late as 1930 had only 1000 subscribers" (190). Thus, textbooks become a crucial source for considering the place of reading in composition.

Composition textbooks were predated by rhetorics, readers, and grammars. Connors notes that rhetoric books before 1800 were not textbooks, but rather treatises that had no pedagogical apparatus. Teachers were entirely responsible for developing pedagogies around these treatises, most of which depended upon the lecture. Connors (1986) locates the 1829 stereotyped edition of Hugh Blair's *Lectures on Rhetoric and Belles-Lettres* as the first textbook because it contained "copious questions and an analysis of each lecture by Abraham Mills, Teacher of Rhetoric" (Connors 1986, 181). These questions promoted little more than rote memorization of certain parts of Blair's lectures. Many rhetorics after this edition included selections accompanied by questions and were used initially at the secondary school level and then in colleges, as well. "Grammars" could be considered "genealogical forebears of today's rhetorical handbooks, combining rules for correct usage and highly condensed advice on writing" (Carr, Carr, and Schultz 2005, 31–32) while "readers," which emerged from "century-old compilations of classical or religious texts and from an eighteenth-century elocutionary tradition of oral performance of written texts" (19) focused primarily, although not exclusively, on reading aloud, including enunciation, pronunciation, and delivery.

When used in colleges, the earliest rhetorics "were taught in a lecture-and-question format, which essentially demanded that students take careful notes on the material and be able on demand to spit it back by rote" (Connors 1997, 71). Early readers such as Lindley Murray's *English Reader* (1799) and Cobb's *Juvenile Reader* (1831) often borrowed heavily from rhetorics, and specifically from British rhetoricians Thomas Sheridan, John Walker, and Hugh Blair. These readers would reprint orations, religious texts, short essays, and other pieces for students to deliver orally. Perhaps the most well-known readers, which were published a bit later in the nineteenth century, are the McGuffey Series, a graduated series of readers for students at all levels, the first of which was published in 1836. William Holmes McGuffey, who edited just the first four readers, was a teacher, administrator, and lecturer. McGuffey's "Eclectic Readers," as they were called, were known for printing a wide range of selections for practice in elocution and are representative of the tradition of readers in that the focus was primarily on delivery, including articulation, pronunciation, as well as the correct posture of the student delivering the oration. Students were taught how to read the symbols that would help them determine the appropriate inflection for each word or phrase. Thus, the reading instruction students received in McGuffey readers, as well as other widely-circulating readers, was largely confined to instruction in elocution.

Because reading was defined in this way, reading instruction was actually instruction in performance. In these readers, the artistic aspect of reading took precedent over other aspects that may have been valued. Although these readers often included complex texts, in most textbooks, it mattered less that students actually understood the material they were reciting and more that they were enunciating and carrying themselves in an appropriate manner. Because the performance, or the "art of reading," as it was called by many textbooks, trumped an understanding of the content, the materials printed in the readers were often redacted or taken out of context since their primary purpose had little to do with their meaning. Paragraphs and even single sentences were plucked from longer works of literature, treatises, and documents from a range of disciplines. Miles Myers (1996, 71) calls this the period of "recitation literacy," that "established textual meaning as familiar, formulaic, memorized, preannounced, delivered and predefined . . . [and] established that learning new meanings was an act of elocution in which messages were digested and assimilated." For the most part, this approach disallowed attention to practices of reading beyond those connected to the delivery of written texts. Thus, instruction in reading was shaped by rhetoric's roots in orality. It is in later readers that we see a shift toward sustained attention not just to orality and the performative aspects of reading, but to instruction in reading as a silent, text-based practice.

It was in the mid-nineteenth century that the move toward universal common school education[1] led to the inclusion of composition within school curricula and "language instruction was expanding its scope to include not just reading and memorizing and parsing text, but also composing text" (Schultz 1999, 21). While in earlier textbooks, "writing" was synonymous with "handwriting," in composition textbooks writing begins to take on the meaning that we ascribe to it today, although, as Schultz points out, "well into the nineteenth century, composition was a critical term that, while carrying a wide range of meanings, especially in the scope of the knowledge and the work that the practice entailed, often signaled a particular feature of a text or a characteristic attached to composing a text, whether oral or written" (148). Textbooks emerged to support instruction in composition, and these books needed to meet the needs of instructors who, for the most part, were inexperienced since "between 1890 and 1910 enrollments practically doubled" (Brereton 1996, 7) and colleges had many more students than experienced instructors from which to draw. Although traditional rhetoric teachers found this shift to simpler, practice- and exercise-based books disheartening, as Connors (1997, 85) points out, "composition instructors were more and more being drawn from the ranks of graduate students, lecturers, and younger assistant professors, and these less-prepared teachers could not take a treatise-style book into a classroom with guaranteed success." Thus, the textbook industry catered to this staffing issue, which meant offering the simplest pedagogical plan possible, including a plethora of drills and exercises to help support these inexperienced instructors.

The face of the student attending college was also changing, and this affected the writing and reading pedagogies instructors could employ. Students were coming from different classes, different geographical locations, and uneven preparations. They were no longer only attending college to take positions in the law or church, and the curriculum had to accommodate. This new population did not have the resources that previous generations of students had and they could not be expected to write on abstract subjects such as Virtue or Justice, which had previously been the norm: "Having been trained only in the vernacular language, classical illustrations and examples were denied him. Commonplace books had faded out . . . without commonplace books, students had no immediate personal access to impersonal knowledge" (Connors 1997, 312). Instructors needed assignments that would not put students at this disadvantage and would not assume that they had a shared knowledge base. Thus, personal experience assignments were born. These assignments filled the pages of composition textbooks published in the late nineteenth century, often replacing the more abstract assignments of earlier years. Emphasizing description and narration (from personal experience), these textbooks highlighted these two modes of discourse at the expense of argument and persuasion, which for years had taken precedent because they were more closely aligned with rhetoric.

Whereas earlier assignments might have asked students to consult sources (e.g., other books, commonplace books, and so on) these assignments asked students to consult themselves, their senses, their abilities of observation, and their reflective capacities. This moment signifies an increasing gap between the teaching of reading and writing. Written composition becomes something wholly separate from reading as students need not look outside of themselves in order to write. Although personal assignments flourished, they never dominated the landscape as there was still a debate as to which subjects were most productive for students to write about, a debate that, of course, continues today.

As is well-known, Harvard was even making significant curricular modifications to adapt to these staffing and population changes. Because of the low scores students were receiving on the written component of their entrance exam, in 1874 Harvard developed the first known freshman composition course called English A, a course that offered exclusive instruction in writing. Many colleges and universities across the country soon followed Harvard's lead. There was, however, at least one exception to this course focused exclusively on written composition, namely Thomas Lounsbury's literature-based composition class, which he first taught at Yale in 1870. His was a model that many colleges followed, particularly those that disagreed with the Harvard model. Reflecting on his pedagogical philosophy in *Harper's Monthly* in 1911, Lounsbury describes writing, which he says, like "painting and sculpture[,] is an imitative art." Lounsbury continues, "To become thoroughly conversant with the work of a great writer, to be influenced by his method of giving utterance to his ideas, to feel profoundly the power and beauty of his style, is worth more for the development of expression than the mastery of all the rhetorical rules that were ever invented" (qtd. in Brereton 1996, 279). Like Lounsbury, William Lyon Phelps, also at Yale, agreed that the teaching of rhetoric in this manner was passé and that reading great literature was the key to developing strong writing skills, an argument that would reappear in the 1980s and continues to be put forth by some scholars today. In his piece entitled "English Composition," published in *Teaching in School and College*, Phelps (1912, 127) writes, "I am certain, however, that the best way to learn to write is to read . . . a student who loves good reading, who has a trained critical taste, will almost always write well, and is in a position to develop his style by practice, the reading and ideas having come in the proper order, first instead of last." It is worth noting that reading was also often touted as integral to the study of writing because—as Phelps points out just above—it could help improve students' taste. This latter benefit would be revisited by the New Critics who, in textbooks such as *Understanding Poetry*, aimed to give students the critical tools they needed in order to differentiate between "good" and "bad" poetry.

Not only would the taste issue re-emerge in the twentieth century, but the conceit that all students need to do is read more in order to become better writers and thinkers—as

Phelps's comment above suggests—remains a trope throughout later scholarship (as well as mainstream media) even today. Like Phelps who described this seemingly automatic improvement in writing as a result from simply reading more, Gerald Thorson, in a 1953 panel discussion, detailed below, noted that college students' "writing will be better; for somehow—I know not how, the study of literature results in many things unexpected" (Thorson 1953, 42). This refrain—that simply assigning reading (and particularly the reading of canonical texts) will *automatically* improve students' writing abilities is practically the foundation upon which Great Books courses and programs depend. But, as Mariolina Salvatori (1996a, 187) would remind us, "To foreground and to teach—rather than just to understand—that interconnectedness [between reading and writing] is a highly constructed, unnatural and obtrusive activity. In other words, nothing is automatic. Students do not somehow learn to write—perhaps by osmosis—simply by reading. Instead, it is the instructor's job to deliberately and consistently "foreground and teach" the connections between reading and writing.

The relationship Salvatori describes between reading and writing would feel even more unnatural to instructors who imagined themselves as teaching literature (rather than the process of reading) and writing. In the early twentieth century, literature played an important role in composition courses. Warner Taylor's 1929 report, "A National Survey of the Conditions in Freshman English," reprinted in Brereton's *The Origins of Composition Studies*, indicates that 107 out of 225 institutions integrated composition and literature instruction in some form and 51 of these made use of literature in one third or more of the instruction in their composition classes. The geographic location of the institution seems to have impacted its approach to the teaching of composition as in the Eastern and Southern states such integration was more common than in Midwest and Western parts of the country. Based on Taylor's data, seventy percent of colleges and universities in the East and fifty percent in the South included literature in their composition courses while around twenty-three percent of schools in the Midwest and West did so (Brereton 1996, 545–562).

The fact that literature was used in composition is important to this study on reading because it provides insight into the reading approaches that circulated in classrooms at the time. At this point, the earlier tradition that rejected rhetorical reading strategies as antiquated was replaced by belletristic approaches to literature. These "assume not only that literary invention is the product of a mysterious mental process but also that the reader needs no hermeneutic with which to interpret the ideas and sentiments that emerge" since methods of reading literary texts were "based on intuiting or admiring the genius of the writer" (Harrington 1997, 255). It was not long, however, before this work was confined to literature classrooms as courses devoted specifically and exclusively to writing were becoming standard practice across the country. James Murphy (1982, 3) describes the establishment of this artificial separation that still exists today as a "ridiculous situation." He explains: "One set of teachers is appointed to teach us how to read, while a second set tries to teach us how to write . . . in virtually every [English] department there is a deeply rooted division between those who teach 'reading,' commonly called 'literature,' and those who teach 'writing,' commonly called 'composition.'" Without rhetoric to hold the practices of reading and writing together, the specialization that Murphy describes only increased as English continued to define itself as a discipline. Educators Nelson and Calfee (1998, 8) describe this process: "As scholarship became more specialized, criticism was being attached to literature, and literary criticism was being established as a separate component of English. Even though some critical study was still included in composition courses, textual criticism was developing apart from any connection to students' own writing. Literature scholars were becoming responsible for the reading of texts, and those in composition were becoming responsible for the writing of texts." Nowhere is this shift more visible than in the rise of the New Criticism in the 1930s. The overwhelming popularity of this theoretical-critical-pedagogical formation in the 1940s and 1950s seems to have cemented the idea that attending to reading fell within the domain of literary studies, not composition.

THE RISE OF THE NEW CRITICISM AND CLOSE READING[2]

The New Critics are perhaps the most well-known intellectuals in history committed to theorizing and teaching reading. I. A. Richards' (1929) *Practical Criticism*, which grew out of his famous experiment wherein he removed the authors' names from pieces of poetry and asked his students to interpret and rank the poems, was one of the first texts to emphasize the problems surrounding the process of making meaning from texts. Cleanth Brooks and Robert Penn Warren's *Understanding Poetry*, described by Arthur Applebee (1974, 163) as the "single most important influence in transforming such critical theory into classroom practice," developed a reading pedagogy to correct the poor reading habits of students that Richards' experiments seemed to corroborate. Brooks and Warren (1950, xiii) describe their goal as follows in the textbook's "Letter to the Teacher": "It is hoped that the juxtaposition of good and bad poems, and of new and old poems, will serve to place emphasis on the primary matter of critical reading and evaluation." The method that was integral to arriving at these judgments was, of course, "close reading," which Brooks and Warren describe as embodying the following three principles: "1. Emphasis should be kept on the poem as a poem 2. The treatment should be concrete and inductive 3. A poem should always be treated as an organic system of relationships, and the poetic quality should never be understood as inhering in one or more factors taken in isolation" (ix).

Alan Golding (1995) has estimated that between 1936 and 1975, 597,940 copies of *Understanding Poetry* were published with its impact most forcefully felt through its first two editions. "The New Critical canon found its way," writes Golding, "especially at the level of method, into a lot of classrooms" (105). Brooks, Warren, and other New Critics' reading pedagogy, which popularized[3] the practice of close reading, continues to inform reading in English Departments today. Even Paul de Man, whose philosophies—outlined in *Allegories of Reading* (1979)—greatly differed from those of the New Critics, couldn't help but reflect on the lasting effect of the New Criticism: "Very little has happened in American criticism since the innovative works of New Criticism" (4). More recently, in Robert Penn Warren's 1989 obituary ("Robert Penn Warren, Poet and Author, Dies" 1989), published in *The New York Times*, *Understanding Poetry* and *Understanding Fiction* (1943) are described as making "the New Criticism dominant in the decade surrounding World War II" and "teaching an entire generation how to read a work of literature." This impact was crucial to the future of English. Whereas the sciences, for example, had a clear subject and thus a reason for existence within academia, this was not the case with English. While New Critics protested (perhaps a bit too much) that they had not modeled their methods after the more "objective" sciences, it worked, and many scholars, including Terry Eagleton (1983, 250), have argued that the New Critics are responsible for the survival of English Departments: "No subsequent movement within English studies has come near to recapturing the courage and radicalism of [the New Critics'] stand. In the early 1920s it was desperately unclear why English was worth studying at all; by the early 1930s it had become a question of why it was worth wasting your time on anything else. English was not only a subject worth studying, but *the* supremely civilizing pursuit, the spiritual essence of the social formation." As Brooks and Warren were publishing the first and second editions of their bestselling textbooks *Understanding Poetry* and *Understanding Fiction*, which extended the reach of the New Criticism by leaps and bounds, the field of composition was defining itself not just in relation to literary studies, but in relation to communication skills, a field that emerged as part of what Connors (1997, 204) calls the "postwar communications movement." In terms of curricula, this meant an increased focus on language and communication and "emphasized the difficulties inherent in skillful use of language with a concomitant need for close, analytical study if the reader or listener were not to be misled" (Applebee 1974, 140). Communication was seen as a skill necessary to keeping peace throughout the world, not only in light of the First World War but in the face of the Second World War, a point Lennox Grey (1943, 12–13), second vice-president of the National Council of Teachers of English, made: "Communication is one of the five or six most crucial services of war. It is one with which a half-dozen major agencies in Washington are now urgently concerned, for home front and battle front alike, following the first imperative concern with military mobilization and war production. It is plainly the one in which our seventy-five thousand teachers of English can make the special war contribution we have been looking, hoping, waiting for." The field was picking up so much momentum that by the end of the 1940s, the word "communication" found its way into the name of what has now become composition's (not communication's) professional organization, the Conference on College Composition and Communication, founded in 1949. The title of the organization speaks to this historical moment in which instruction in the communication arts, including reading, writing, speaking, and listening was taking off. This movement offered a more comprehensive approach to literacy instruction, reminiscent in certain ways of rhetoric. In fact, John C. Gerber who helped organize CCCCs suggested that it was the communication skills programs that reinvigorated interest in rhetoric within English: "The revival of interest in rhetoric began, really, in our composition classes in the late 1940s with the great emphasis at the time on communication skills. . . . In their short life they broke up the notion of the successful composition as a static discourse needing only unity, coherence, and emphasis for its success" (qtd. in Crowley 1998, 183). A. M. Tibbets, however, commented on how "rhetoric was 'crowded out' of the course by its teachers' inadequate level of preparedness and the general level of confusion that emanated from communication skills programs" (qtd. in Crowley 1998, 184). The communication skills movement was short-lived, and most communication skills programs were phased out by 1960 (Crowley 1998, 183). Still, the communication skills movement had enough of an impact to provoke Brooks and Warren to develop a pedagogy that challenged its foundations, which treated literature and poetry as acts of communication, rather than treating *literature as literature* and *poetry as poetry* as the New Criticism demanded.

Because the New Criticism had practically taken over literary studies altogether, which was now heavily invested in reading, composition began to associate itself more with linguistics and discourse studies. Still, as Dana Harrington (1997, 258) points out, justifications for teaching literature that abound at the 1948 meeting of NCTE reveal "the extent to which literary analysis dominated the curriculum of English departments [including that of composition classes] even as composition studies was attempting to distance itself from literature." Questions raised and arguments made in essays published in the newly founded professional journal *College Composition and Communication* during this time, as well as comments made during professional meetings support the ambivalence that composition felt toward the teaching of reading, which was often conflated with literature, as it still is today. Consider the following excerpts:

> "Is there any room in the elementary composition course for the study of *literature as literature*—in the sense of belles lettres?" There is not very much room! If *literature as literature* is to be studied at all, it should be limited in amount; it should come late in the course; and it should be clearly designated for what it is—something apart, essentially, from the central material of the course. (Workshop 3A [1950] *College Composition and Communication*, 12)

> Literature should be taught *as literature*, even in Freshman English. (Gerald Thorson [1953], "Literature in Freshman English," *College Composition and Communication*, 88, emphasis added)

> The method of using complete literary works was an essential part of the success of the [freshman composition] course. (Wayne Booth [1956], "Imaginative Literature is Indispensable," *College Composition and Communication*, 37)

> We should make sure that the student is introduced to some
> of the great masterpieces of literature, in all their richness and
> depth; we must open up for him the world of literature. We do
> not achieve this by having him read Mr. Hayakawa's chapter on
> literature, but by having him read *literature itself*. (Gerald Thorson
> [1956], "Literature: The Freshman's Key," *College Composition and
> Communication*, 40, emphasis added)

The New Critical directives to treat literature *as literature*, to
work with whole texts, and to read literature *itself* rather than
to read *about* literature clearly inform the above excerpts. In
fact, in its first ten issues, *College Composition and Communication*
published several articles on the place of literature and reading
instruction within composition, and in 1955 ran a series entitled
"The Teaching of Reading in the Freshman Course." This new
group of professionals who began to see themselves as experts in
writing instruction were ambivalent about how the New Critical
theories should affect their classroom practices. This ambivalence, of course, anticipates a similar reaction registered in the
scholarship on reading that re-emerges in the 1980s and 1990s,
and most directly in the Lindemann-Tate debate, discussed in
the introduction and the following chapter. Gerald Thorson,
quoted above, actually went on to qualify his comments that
at first suggest he aligns himself entirely with the New Critics.
Clarifying his statement that literature should be taught as literature, Thorson (1953, 38) notes: "To deny [literature's] value
as a means of communication is to ignore one of the traditional
sources of communication." Thorson creates a scenario in which
Freshman English treats literature as literature *and* as communication. Thorson describes the teaching of reading in composition—which he touches on only briefly—in terms of its relationship to communication as he notes that "through literature a
Freshman English instructor can teach the methods of getting at
what is communicated. Reading and understanding are valuable
goals in communication." For Thorson, though, the primary use
of literature is not to teach reading, but rather to "furnish ideas
for class discussion and writing" (38), a commonly held position
by contemporary writing instructors, as well.

DISCUSSIONS OF THE PLACE OF READING IN
COMPOSITION AT EARLY CCCCS MEETINGS

The professional discourse surrounding the place of reading instruction took off in the spring of 1954 when a panel discussion on the topic was held at the meeting of the Conference on College Composition and Communication in St. Louis. The participants included Chairman James I. Brown, University of Minnesota; Russell Cosper, Purdue University; J. Hooper Wise, University of Florida; and discussion leader Alton Hobgood, Georgia Institute of Technology. An overview of the papers presented by the panelists was published by E. J. Hutchinson, the recorder at the Convention, in *College Composition and Communication* the following year under the series title "The Teaching of Reading in the Freshman Course." The spring 1955 meeting of the CCCCs, held in Chicago, hosted a panel on the related topic "The Place of Literature in Freshman English." The papers presented by Wayne Booth, Earlham College; Gerald Thorson, Augsburg College; Harrison Hayford, Northwestern University; and Gladys K. Brown, Little Rock Junior College were published in *College Composition and Communication* in 1956. The papers ultimately demonstrate that compositionists often got caught up in the service aspect of the composition course as they considered how and why reading instruction should complement writing instruction. For example, Hutchinson (1955, 94) reports that the panelists discussed the following important purpose which instruction in reading served: "To increase general reading efficiency, to increase reading interest and appreciation, to improve the level of comprehension through critical reading with concerns for logic and semantics, to train to adjust speed to the type of material being read." Although the panel uses the term "critical reading," which circulates in the 1980s and 1990s and still today, within this much earlier context the term is associated with comprehension. The panel also emphasized the importance of speed in reading and Cosper described how Purdue University offered a reading laboratory program that enrolled 638 students whose primary problem with reading was the speed with which they read (in addition to—although to a lesser degree it seems—their comprehensive abilities). For the most part, reading instruction is defined as remedial work and, as such, the compositionists seem to suggest, it should be attended to in the composition classroom or in some extension of that class-room, such as a reading laboratory. It would seem that com-positionists themselves, thus, become partly responsible for perpetuating the field's association with basic skills from which composition has consistently tried to extricate itself. Many of the characterizations of reading that emerge in Hutchinson's recording of the session are the very ones that Brooks and Warren, and the New Critics, more generally, were working against, including the speed-reading movement and reading for appreciation only.

The papers presented in 1955 on the "Place of Literature in the Freshman Course" as part of Workshop 3 at the Conference on College Composition and Communication also suggest that the topic was the site of much contention. Moreover, as Harrison Hayford (1956, 42), one of the panelists noted, "The traditional course which combines composition and literature, as the basic freshman course, has been under pressure during the past ten years or so." Hayford lays out the two positions he imagines in the debate. On the one side are those who argue that the "basic freshman course" should be restricted to com-munication skills, which would include a focus on reading and writing, and would give the course a "subject matter of its own" (43), a position that would be furthered by American schol-ars at the Dartmouth Seminar, discussed below. On the other side are those who believe that these are remedial skills that should have been dealt with earlier in students' educations and, as such, the "basic course" should be *primarily* a litera-ture course . . . great books by great writers" (43, emphasis in original). Hayford locates the answer to this dilemma between the two poles, describing how Northwestern—his school— offers a course "which tries to pay attention to the imperatives of both of the movements" (45). The split described above is characterized by the basic skills approach we saw furthered by the compositionists on the "The Teaching of Reading in the Freshman Course" panel and by those who rejected what they deemed remediation in favor of the study of literature. Drawing on his investments in rhetoric (and on Kenneth Burke's influence, who Wayne Booth deemed "the most important living critic"), Booth, then teaching at Earlham College, also on the panel, supports what he calls "the use of properly chosen imaginative literature" since it "produces results in the thinking, speaking, and writing of the majority of the students that nothing else can produce so well." Booth offers the important caveat, though, that "learning to appreciate literature is not a substitute for learning how to write" (Booth 1956, 35). For Booth, literature can be capitalized on in the composition classroom because of its *difficulty*, a term that Mariolina Salvatori's reading pedagogy will depend upon as she introduces it in the 1980s. Booth explains, "Only if our entering students were already deeply interested in improving their writing, only if they knew how to read complicated expository and imaginative prose, could we dispense with the value of literature as a vehicle, as a tool" (36). Whereas others on the panel argued that students who read good literature automatically became strong writers: "the writing will be better; for somehow—I know not how, the study of literature results in many things unexpected" (Thorson 1953, 42), Booth's investment in using literature hinges on a more specific rendering of how literature enables professors to offer instruction in reading difficult texts. In Booth's terms, literature is a tool that not only helps students to write, but that simultaneously offers support in the connected practice of reading "complicated expository and imaginative prose." Although rare at the time, Booth's approach does not involve choosing between reading instruction (often considered narrowly in terms of remediation) and literary study. Instead, Booth considers the important intersections between the practices of reading and writing and ultimately calls for the deliberate use of literature to teach reading.

THE SHIFTING DISCUSSION: FROM
READING TO LITERATURE

Despite Booth's position, articles arguing that the field of composition was the appropriate site for attention to remedial reading instruction continued to abound in the professional discourse. In *College English*'s "Teach Us To Read," for example, William D. Baker acknowledges that while the author's diction, vocabulary, tone, and the meaning of the reading are all worth stressing, it is equally important to help students "adjust[t] one's rate of reading." To omit this aspect of reading instruction, argues Baker, is "to leave the job half-done" (Baker 1953, 232). Baker makes the case that teachers of Freshman English should be responsible for helping students to read "faster and more efficiently" (233) and that it does not matter that these instructors have no technical or formal training in reading instruction since neither do they have formal training in teaching composition. Baker argues that the goal would be to increase the speed at which students read without diminishing their comprehension. In the course he is calling for, "writing might still have the most time allotted to it, but developmental reading, intelligently dovetailed into the writing program would take a significant position" (233).

Although articles on reading instruction in the composition classroom would decline, *College Composition and Communication* continued to publish pieces on the place of literature in the composition classroom. Natalie Calderwood (University of Kansas) would revisit the subject in her talk at the March 1957 Conference on College Composition and Communication, which was published under the title "Composition and Literature" the same year in *College Composition and Communication*. A year later, John A. Hart, Robert C. Stack, and Neal Woodruff, Jr. (Carnegie Institute of Technology) would do the same in their article entitled "Literature in the Composition Course" (Hart, Stack, and Woodruff 1958). The shift, as it is represented by these articles and those published by *College Composition and Communication* and *College English* into the 1960s, is toward considering the role of literature—not reading instruction—in the mid-century composition classroom. Albert Kitzhaber's groundbreaking survey of freshman composition programs at close to one hundred colleges and universities in 1959–1960 also documented the place of literature (not reading instruction) in the composition classroom, concluding that at approximately twenty percent of the institutions he studied courses combined literary studies and composition instruction.

Kitzhaber's next study would be published in what has been called a watershed year for composition—1963. Not only was this the year that Kitzhaber's study of freshman programs, including Dartmouth's—*Themes, Theories, and Therapy*—was published, but it was the year that the annual CCCC meeting shifted its focus to the relationship between composition and rhetoric, accounting for what some have called the revival of rhetoric (Kitzhaber 1963). More than fifteen hundred attended the meeting, which exceeded attendance at earlier meetings (Connors 1997, 206), and many of the panels and workshops focused on the relationship between composition and rhetoric.

COMPOSITION, EDUCATION, AND COMMUNICATION SKILLS PROGRAMS

While composition was considering the resources offered by classical rhetoric, the field was simultaneously trying to separate itself from communications programs, a split which Francis Bowman, outgoing CCCC chair, addressed in 1962 (Trimbur and George 1999, 55). Most important for this study, though, is how attention to reading instruction at this moment in which composition is overtly defining its scope begins to migrate to other disciplines. Although composition does not begin to neglect reading instruction entirely, attention to reading would seem to move toward the margins of composition and find homes elsewhere, including in education and even communications. While this is not the place to explore in-depth the various fields to which research in reading instruction seemed to migrate, it is worth quickly glossing how the fields of education and communications, in particular, began staking out this territory as composition focused less and less on reading instruction.

The publication of Rudolf Flesch's (1955) *Why Johnny Can't Read—and What You Can Do about It* created a stir that led the Carnegie Corporation to fund a study on methods of reading instruction. The study would be conducted from 1962 to 1965 by Jeanne Chall from the field of education whose work on this particular project would lead her to Harvard where she would create and direct a graduate program within education in the field of reading instruction. Her findings were published in 1967 under the title *The Great Debate*. Both before and after the publication of *The Great Debate*, Chall was called on repeatedly to advise public figures, including presidents, on reading instruction within the schools. Although Chall's studies and publications were primarily focused on teaching young children how to read, over the years, her research expanded to include reading instruction for adults and reading instruction in post-secondary settings. All of this is to suggest that around the time that composition was seeking to define itself, the field of education was quickly becoming the arena in which questions surrounding reading instruction were being considered. Because of the public nature of Chall's work and those who would follow, education was emerging as the public face of research in reading.

More surprising, though, is how in "Wired for Sound: Teaching, Communications, and Technological Culture," Walter J. Ong notes that, "if students are losing their hold on reading and grammar, this is in part because, in their relationship to the other items involved in communication, reading and grammar are not what they used to be (Ong 1960, 247). Ong's focus on reading and how new technologies necessarily affect reading instruction and grammar instruction proves relevant. Composition's rejection of communications around this time— the very field that was asking questions about new technologies and their effects on literacy—meant that composition was no longer aligned with the field that would be taking up these reading-related questions.

THE DARTMOUTH SEMINAR ON THE TEACHING OF ENGLISH

Another arena in which members of English Departments were working to define English's disciplinary subject and boundaries, including the place of its subfields such as composition, was the Dartmouth Seminar on the Teaching of English that brought together approximately fifty prominent American and British scholar-teachers. They met for three weeks in the summer of 1966 for this seminar, which was funded by the Carnegie Corporation and organized by the MLA, the NCTE, and the British National Association for Teachers of English. As Joseph Harris has done before me, I look to the Dartmouth Seminar not to mark "an heroic shift in the theory and practice of teaching" since "the work of most teachers in America and Britain, from preschool to the university, seems only too often to have continued on after Dartmouth much as it had before—marching lockstep to the demands of fixed school curriculums, standardized tests, and calls for improved skills and increased cultural unity" (Harris 1997, 2–3). Instead, I point to the seminar as bringing to the fore—as did the workshops and early meetings of the Conference on Composition and Communication in the 1950s—the conflicts surrounding the role of reading in composition instruction.

The Dartmouth Seminar, which consisted of presentations, workshops, and study groups, has been studied—as have the reports and other documents that emerged from it—by many scholars. I rehearse the well-known background as quickly as I can in order to move on to an exploration of how this seminar can serve as a resource for considering how reading instruction and the New Criticism were being discussed within the context of composition at this moment. It would seem that the most accurate representations of the seminar take into account the range of philosophies that made coming to a consensus concerning the teaching of English difficult, if not impossible. Participants set out to explore the question "What is English?" and did so by considering the entirety of the English curriculum from kindergarten all the way through post-secondary education. Albert Kitzhaber who presented the first paper at the conference, addressed the topic through what he saw as the three branches of English, namely, language, literature, and composition. He argued that these areas of interest needed to be better integrated in order to create "an organized body of knowledge" (Kitzhaber 1966, 12). His argument, which is fairly representative of the American scholars' position, ultimately envisioned English as needing a proper subject not unlike the other disciplines (e.g., the sciences): "It will be part of the concern of this seminar to decide whether there must be and in fact is a subject-matter 'center' for the English curriculum and what that center consists of; or whether there is no single identifiable center" (16).

Although this focus on the proper *subject* of English is reminiscent of debates around the turn of the century, the "American" approach was in stark contrast to the position of many of the English scholars. James Britton, the official discussant at Kitzhaber's presentation, wanted to focus, instead, on what he called "areas of experience in which the language-structuring-experience process would operate; or in terms of the frames of reference (including the bodies of knowledge) which it is hoped will result from such a process" (Kitzhaber 1966, 2). The two approaches, represented by Kitzhaber and Britton, primarily differ in how they imagine the English curriculum: the American scholars largely wanted to approach the curriculum through its content whereas the English scholars were more concerned with how the curriculum might reflect a commitment to process, particularly how students process and structure their experiences. As such, Britton reframed the question "What is English?" that Kitzhaber was attempting to answer, and, instead, asked: "What ought English teachers to be doing?"

This focus on process led the English scholars, and Britton, in particular, to introduce pedagogies—particularly composition pedagogies—that we take for granted today, but were new at the time. First, Britton spent time in his response to Kitzhaber exploring the connections between the processes of reading and writing, using the sort of language that American composition scholars in the 1980s would adopt. Arguing for the use of "language to learn" [or] "an operational view of language," Kitzhaber (1966, 9) describes what happens when a student writes: "He copies with [sic] experience he has been writing about by shaping it in words and the writing may be the act of perceiving the shape of experience—not the evidence that it has been perceived, but the act of perceiving it." The same goes for reading: "Whenever he successfully reads something which has tested his ability, strains his ability, he has coped with experience. . . . He has shaped experience—entered into and altered and shaped experience—and has also improved his skill, his ability to read a difficult passage" (9). The emphasis Britton places on difficulty as a tool that foregrounds the composing process and helps students to actively shape and understand their experiences echoes Booth's position, discussed earlier, and anticipates the work that scholars such as David Bartholomae, Anthony Petrosky, Mariolina Salvatori, and Patricia Donahue will undertake decades later. Moreover, Britton's connecting the processes of reading and writing—both as acts of composing meaning within the text, as well as within one's experience—also anticipate the work of these important American scholars and underscores the emphasis that English scholars were already placing on this particular understanding of reading instruction. This philosophy was in contrast to the American scholars' largely content-driven arguments like those Kitzhaber makes regarding the need to unify English around a "subject."

Grammar proved a sticking point for the two camps with many of the English scholars (with the exception of the English linguists) wanting to minimize the systematic teaching of language and grammar. According to Muller, they "pointed out that there was no evidence to support the assumption that systematic teaching of language improved writing." They were content, instead, to rely on students' unconscious mastery of the language and would introduce such lessons "only the when the need arises from the work of the class" (Muller 1967, 70). Opposed to what was termed an "implicit way of teaching," American scholars argued for the consistent use of grammar exercises and more explicit and consistent instruction in language, which they viewed as humanistic (71–72). Muller drew up a statement that explained this position: "[Students] should be made aware of the fluidity of language, variations in English, the existence of dialects, difference in standards, and the basis for standards." This was all in the service of the necessity of the student "learning to speak and write 'good English.'" Muller continues, "The fundamental importance of language in man's realizing his humanity and carrying on all his distinctive activities makes it desirable that the student have some awareness of this importance, and so far as possible some knowledge of the nature, structure, and history of English" (72). By focusing on what they saw as the relationship between language and humanist studies, the American scholars laid the groundwork for their argument for unifying the subject of English.

As its title indicates, the third paper of the opening session, "What is Teachable in Composition and How?" (Kitzhaber 1966, 2), addresses more specific questions related to composition pedagogy. The paper critiques the "typical form of the freshman course" in which students "write 'papers' on a variety of subjects and in a variety of modes" because "in practice, the papers are little more than means of testing the students' command of the mechanics of the written language." In place of these exercises in the proper and accurate use of language, the paper proposes "for the modern composition teacher a role somewhat like that filled by Socrates" in which the teacher does not provide answers but "direct[s] discussion so that answers may be found" (12). The composition teacher must "conceive his students as being engaged, when they write, in a process" (12) and help them develop some sense of how to find the answers to the problems that writers face, how to make the decisions that writers make (12–13). The speaker goes on to describe how this approach translates into practice with the use of drafts, which he concedes may seem like "an excessively long and tedious process to produce so small a thing as a student paper. But so far as we know anything about the productive activities of writers, we seem to see that they do go through quite as tedious and long a process. And insofar as students have come under our observation in this context, we are surely all aware that their writing process is truncated either in its parts or in the time given to it" (14). This comparison of student writing to professional writing, and thus the impulse to develop a process-driven pedagogy that more accurately reflected the work of professional writers, was a common trope throughout the English scholars' papers. In his account of the seminar, *Growth through English*, John Dixon (1975, 10) emphasizes the importance of associating composition with a process rather than a finished product by thinking about "the activity of bringing together and composing the disorder of our experiences." While the emphasis on process and drafting may no longer seem groundbreaking, the Dartmouth Seminar was a site that introduced these ideas to American scholars.

The participants at the Dartmouth Seminar couldn't help but address the New Criticism. Despite their different emphases, the English and American scholars agreed, according to Muller (1967, 86) in *The Uses of English*, that "the New Critics were too schematic and called for too much explicit analysis, which again amounted to learning about literature and might interfere with the enjoyment of it, the direct personal response of the student." While both sides "appreciated the New Critics stress on aesthetic values and closer reading," they found the New Critical focus on strictly formal properties of texts too narrow and many of the English participants called, instead, for a more interdisciplinary approach to counteract the narrowness of the New Critical approach.

At the Dartmouth Seminar and beyond it was slowly becoming clear that just as early elocutionary readers "established that learning new meanings was an act of elocution in which messages were [already] digested and assimilated" (Myers 1996, 71), the New Critics "established textual meaning as familiar, formulaic, memorized [and] preannounced." Years later, David Bartholomae (1996, 245) would characterize this position as follows: "[The New Criticism] marked a potentially positive moment of intervention in the English curriculum, one that would redefine the relationship between the student and the text . . . but the potential of the moment was lost when the classroom exercise became not only formalistic . . . but also elitist (a celebration of the 'genius' of the author and a necessary subordination of students and their writing before 'primary writing.') The subject in the curriculum became someone else's reading and writing, someone bigger, better, more famous, more powerful."

While compositionists weren't sold on the New Criticism, the field embraced some of the theoretical responses to the New Criticism, including reader-response theory and feminist theory since both authorized and empowered readers rather than texts. In fact, a great deal of the scholarship that would eventually call for the deliberate integration of reading in the composition classroom and in the discipline more broadly builds upon the reader-response approach that places the reader (which would become the student in composition scholarship) at its center. As the next chapter considers in great detail, some of the key players in the discussions about the place of reading in composition draw explicitly on these theories. For example, reader-response theory insofar as it "sought to explain what happens when people read," made reading teachable—"as process theories of composing helped to make writing teachable in the eighties" (Harkin 2005, 415). In fact, Harkin points out that "in spite of its very considerable theoretical sophistication, more often than not, reader-response came to be associated, almost exclusively, with pedagogy . . . as compositionists sought to use reader-response theory to teach students to read difficult texts" (419). The readings in David Bartholomae and Anthony Petrosky's (1987, 10) widely circulating composition reader *Ways of Reading* were, in fact, chosen "with the understanding that they were difficult to read." Two of the most prolific compositionists during the 1980s and 1990s (and today), Mariolina Salvatori and Patricia Donahue, also build their reading/writing pedagogy described in their textbook *The Elements (and Pleasures) of Difficulty* around the very concept of difficulty, which they contend is crucial in one's academic career and beyond: "Readers who engage, rather than avoid, a text's difficulties can deepen their understanding of what they read and how they read. If they move away from those difficulties or opt for somebody solving them for them, chances are that they will never know the cause of those difficulties, and the means to control them. And insofar as reading involves thinking—thinking the thoughts of another, inhabiting somebody else's mind—temporarily adopting somebody else's argument—learning to read in ways that nurture flexibility of mind can be good preparation for encountering and working through difficult life situations" (Salvatori and Donahue 2005, 3).[4] These pedagogies, like reader-response theory, de-center the place of the text in reading, which had reached a quasi-religious level in the New Critical approach. Although some of the key reader-response critics, including Louise Rosenblatt whose work finally garnered attention in the 1970s, could not convincingly offer a reconceptualization of the text itself, their challenging of the status of the text alone led "in American educational circles to the development of new teaching practices in which literature was no longer seen as a body of privileged texts whose meanings students must 'understand correctly'" (McCormick 1994, 37). Most important for this study is that with attention focused on readers rather than the previously all-mighty text, the pedagogy that grew out of this shift, turned "readers-as-consumers into readers-as-producers of their own readings of texts" (Comley 1985, 130–1). The process movement, which can be traced to the mid-1970s, supported this changing view of the text and of student-readers. Thanks to early process theorists such as Janet Emig it became more common to consider the challenges of composing as affecting *all* writers, including published ones, rather than just students. As Crowley (1998, 202) explains, previously "students' writing was sharply distinguished in kind from that produced by the poets and novelists they read in class, which was presented to them as though it had been created in an instant by the inspired insight of 'great' minds." With the popularization of process pedagogies, "students themselves, rather than the texts they produced, became the locus of instruction." This emphasis on the writing process also shifted attention toward the reading process, resulting in the publication, sharing, and development of hundreds of essays, textbooks, conference papers, and colloquia devoted to the topic of reading in composition, the very subject of the following chapter.

NOTES

1. At this time, education reformers were pushing to provide universal, public, and free education to all children and to standardize curricula across the schools. This was a response, in part, to the reformers' belief that young children were no longer receiving the education (moral and otherwise) through the traditional institutions that had previously provided it, including parents and churches. Common schools—today's equivalent to elementary schools—were intended to remedy this problem while also aiming to provide an education comparable to the education some children had been receiving in private schools.

2. For an insightful overview of how the New Critics and formalism, more generally, affected the development of the field of composition see Nystrand, Greene, and Wiemelt's (1993) "Where Did Composition Studies Come From?: An Intellectual History."

3. I use the term "popularized" rather than "introduced" because my research indicates that not only did the contemporary textbooks that *Understanding Poetry* claimed to oppose contain this central concern of the New Criticism but textbooks published several decades earlier also advocate close attention to the text above all else. In *Studies in English and American Literature from Chaucer to Present*, for example, Albert Newton Raub (1882) writes that "the study of special biography does not help students appreciate classics or prepare students for authorship" and that the method, instead, should be to "study closely . . . beauties, but also defects" (3) of the readings therein. William Swinton's *Studies in English Literature* derides textbooks that include authors' biographies and in the 1880 preface to this textbook, Swinton (1880) writes that his book will not "cram on the personal biography of authors" like other textbooks, which have students "reading *about* literature" rather than "reading *in* literature" (iii). Slightly later, Martin Wright Sampson's writing on the topic of literary instruction included the directive to place "the student face to face with the work itself" (Graff 2007). My work with these textbooks complicates some of Gerald Graff's arguments made in *Professing Literature* regarding textbooks from the late 1800s. Graff makes a claim for uniformity among textbooks of this time period. This is problematic not only because he covers over the differences that inevitably characterize any set of textbooks, but because this uniformity serves as a straw man to eventually mark revolutionary breaks in the textbook industry.

4. Although not focused on composition, Sheridan Blau's (2003) *The Literature Workshop* also focuses on the importance of teaching difficult texts and Blau emphasizes the teaching of reflective and metacognitive practices, as do Salvatori and Donahue. For more on Blau's book see the annotated bibliography in Appendix A.

4
READING IN COMPOSITION RESEARCH AND TEACHING, 1980–1993

In the 1980s and early 1990s, textbooks, collections of essays, and conferences on the subject of reading (on its own) and on connections between reading and writing were plentiful. The long, but still woefully incomplete list below is intended to indicate the sheer amount of scholarship that emerged from this moment, as well as a few textbooks. Some collections, such as Atkins and Johnson's (1985) *Writing and Reading Differently*, which used deconstruction to explore the relationship between reading and writing, addressed reading-writing connections from theoretical perspectives. Other collections, such as Robert J. Tierney, Patricia L. Anders, and Judy Nichols Mitchell's 1987 collection entitled *Understanding Readers' Understanding: Theory and Practice* included both theoretical and practical perspectives that explored reading practices within the context of writing instruction (Tierney, Anders, and Mitchell 1987). In 1986, the same year that Bruce T. Petersen's (1986) edited collection entitled *Convergences: Transactions in Reading and Writing* was published, the first of David Bartholomae and Anthony Petrosky's textbooks, *Facts, Artifacts, and Counterfacts,* which documented their basic reading and writing course at the University of Pittsburgh, was published. This textbook was followed shortly thereafter, in 1987, by the first edition of *Ways of Reading*.

Several conferences were held and talks on the topic of reading were presented during this time, as well, and essays based on these talks were often published in edited collections. Thomas Newkirk's 1986 collection entitled *Only Connect: Uniting Reading and Writing* features essays based on talks given

DOI: 10.7330/9780874219609.c004

at a 1984 conference at the University of New Hampshire. Ann E. Berthoff, Judith Goleman, David Bartholomae, and Louise Z. Smith (1988) are among those published in that collection. Elizabeth Flynn (1982) presented "Peer Tutoring and Reading Activities" at the 1982 meeting of the Conference on College Composition and Communication. At this point, Flynn (along with John Clifford) was editing and publishing the journal *Reader: Essays in Reader-Oriented Theory, Criticism and Pedagogy* through Michigan Technological University. The journal began in 1976 as a newsletter dedicated to reader-response criticism.[1]

During this time, several articles dedicated to investigating connections between the processes of reading and writing and the relationship between the fields of literature and composition appeared in the field's journals. Although there are far too many articles to list here, those published in *College English* include Alan C. Purves's (1983) "Language Processing: Reading and Writing"; Mariolina Salvatori's (1983) "Reading and Writing a Text: Correlations between Reading and Writing"; and Linda Flower's (1988) "The Construction of Purpose in Writing and Reading". *Rhetoric Review* also published articles on the subject, including Joseph Comprone's (1983) "Recent Research in Reading and Its Implications for the College Composition Classroom"; David Paxman's (1984) "Reinventing the Composition/Literature Course"; Patricia Bizzell's (1986) "On the Possibility of a Unified Theory of Composition and Literature"; and Louise Wetherbee Phelps's (1986) "The Domain of Composition." *College Composition and Communication* published, among others, Donald Murray's (1982) "Teaching the Other Self: The Writer's First Reader"; Christina Haas and Linda Flower's (1988) "Rhetorical Reading Strategies and the Construction of Meaning"; Anthony Petrosky's (1982) "From Story to Essay: Reading and Writing"; and William J. Vande Kopple's (1982) "Functional Sentence Perspective, Composition, and Reading." Also in 1982, Toby Fulwiler and Art Young edited the collection *Language Connections: Writing and Reading across the Curriculum* (Fulwiler and Young 1982). As this still all-too-small sampling is intended to suggest, the place of reading within composition was on many people's minds as compositionists worked to define the field in relation to and against literary studies.

The 1980s and early 1990s marks the one period in the field's history that produced reading-related theories and focused on pedagogical practices to enact them. The tremendous increase in interest in reading pedagogies at the time the discipline was defining itself suggests that there was the potential for this aspect of composition to become one of the field's defining features and a lasting part of its landscape. Yet, it did not. As Chapter 1 notes, histories of the field, such as Stephen North's *The Making of Knowledge in Composition* and more recent anthologies including the *Norton Book of Composition Studies* and *Cross-Talk in Comp Theory: A Reader* overlook this moment. The field's neglect of reading in first-year composition courses over the last two decades leaves not only a theoretical gap in the professional discourse, but ultimately a pedagogical gap. As David Jolliffe (2007), one of the few compositionists that continues to publish on reading, points out: "Because the topic of reading lies outside the critical discourse of composition studies" instructors do "not have access to ample resources to help them think about a model of active constructive reading in the courses or about strategies for putting that model into play" (478).

This chapter argues that the struggle over disciplinary identity may be at the heart of reading's rather quick demise. Extending the argument that the "great divorce" or "great divide"—wherein composition sought to separate itself from literary studies—is responsible for reading's disappearance, this chapter considers how reading, as a subject of inquiry, got caught up in the clashes—disciplinary, political, and others— that characterized English studies and departments at the time. This chapter looks closely at the scholarship from this period, which demonstrates how scholars were working toward different goals as they sought to define composition. The scholarship also exposes slippages between the terms "reading" and "literature," and ultimately conflations of the terms, that, in the end, privilege "literature" and issues related to text selection rather than the process of reading. This chapter views this moment as instructive and filled with potential, but argues that largely because of these differing goals and slippages and conflations, reading did not have a strong enough hold to become one of the field's primary subjects of inquiry.

The disciplinary struggles and the stakes associated with defining and studying reading—at the very moment that scholars were attempting to also define the field of composition in relation to other subfields in English, as well as to other departments such as education, communication, and even psychology—meant that the "reading movement,"[2] was never able to coalesce in ways that may have supported its lasting longer. Historians in the field (e.g., Susan Miller, Thomas Newkirk, Winifred Bryan Horner, Patricia Harkin) offer more in-depth accounts of these struggles, but it is worth noting that some of these clashes included the following: conflicting relations between composition and literary studies; between research and pedagogy; between valuing student texts and published, "literary" texts; between sealing English studies off from other disciplines and valuing interdisciplinarity. In her introduction to *Composition and Literature: Bridging the Gap*, Winifred Bryan Horner (1983, 6) characterizes the clash among the fields of education, composition, and literary studies as follows: "For years [composition research] has been carried on in schools of education and has been largely concerned with pedagogy at the lower school level. Maverick English professors who pursued research in composition theory or the teaching of composition did so at their own peril." Although not explicitly, many departments still, in the 1980s, made it "clear to their junior members [who were hired as compositionists and WPAs] that promotion and tenure would not be awarded on the basis of research in composition [but on research in literary studies]." Richard A. Lanham in the same collection, writes that "Composition was all that English studies had striven for a hundred years not to be. Avowedly a 'service department,' it had no room of its own in theory or in practice. The very opposite of self-enclosed, it served as time and circumstance dictated. Freshman writing,

technical writing, business writing, legal writing—you name
it and comp people would try to do it" (qtd. in Horner 1983,
16). Patricia Harkin 2005 describes the more specific conflicts
within the community of scholars invested in studying reading,
a conflict that also exposes the strained relationship between
research and teaching: "Early reading theorists whose principal
commitment was to literary criticism were at pains to dissociate
themselves from its pedagogical implications . . . as too much
attention to reader-response [theory] might cause us to dwindle
from researchers to teachers" (419).

While most hypotheses explain reading's disappearance by
looking at forces outside of the reading movement such as
"the social turn"[3] or in-depth accounts of the great divorce, this
chapter looks inside the movement by considering the scholarship itself in order to expose the struggle over composition's
disciplinary identity, resulting in the conflation of the terms
"reading" and "literature," as well as the common threads across
this scholarship. And so, this chapter acknowledges *two ways of
reading this scholarship*. The first way locates this scholarship as
indicative of the struggle to define composition as a field and
extends the argument that the "great divorce" is largely responsible for the shift away from reading. The scholarship that this
chapter studies exposes this series of clashes among scholars for
whom there were different stakes and goals associated with how
they went about defining and theorizing reading. Moreover,
many of these scholars were some of the first to earn graduate
degrees in composition and rhetoric as opposed to literature
and so tenure and their jobs were at stake if they could not
prove to their colleagues in their departments that composition was a valid, legitimate, and theoretically rigorous field of
study. In other words, they needed to prove that composition
was more than the teaching of the required freshman English
course. Reading got tangled up in these conflicts as scholars'
perspectives were anchored in different (often competing) versions of composition's emerging identity, disallowing reading
from coalescing as a primary focus of the field. Patricia Harkin
(2005, 421) describes composition in the 1980s as follows:

"It's fair to say that composition studies ultimately saw itself as tainted by reader-response—indeed by all literary theory. What may have begun simply as an effort to shake free from literary studies had the not-always-intended effect of excluding all instruction in reading." She continues, "Because discussions of reading have been so thoroughly conflated with discussions of teaching literature, a decision *not* to teach literary texts in writing courses became or entailed a decision not to teach reading." It is worth noting, too, that related to this hypothesis is the theory that some compositionists were also invested in separating themselves from reading instruction as it was defined by education (particularly K–12) since their colleagues in literary studies were skeptical about how rigorous research in the field of education truly was.

The second way this chapter attends to the scholarship on reading from the 1980s and 1990s is by drawing out the conceptual and theoretical continuities within the scholarship. Ultimately, this work of tracing the unifying threads rather than simply pointing out the problematic slippages within the scholarship proves particularly useful in imagining how this moment in the history of the field might be instructive as we consider the most productive ways of reintroducing reading to composition.

The value that this chapter places on coherence, particularly as it reads the scholarship in this second way, assumes that coherence is not only more valuable than incoherence, but even attainable within any given field or discipline. As does this study, Stephen North (1987, 364) has raised concerns about the lack of coherence of the discipline: "Composition as a knowledge-making society is gradually pulling itself apart. Not branching out or expanding . . . but fragmenting: gathering into communities or clusters of communities among which relations are becoming increasingly tenuous." Robert Connors details these factions in "Rhetorical History as a Component of Composition Studies": "We are already pursuing research paths so disparate that many thoughtful people have feared that the discipline may fly apart like a dollar watch. Social constructivists critique cognitivists. Marxists deride expressionists. Social science-based researchers refuse to cater to 'uninformed readers.' Theorists cannot speak easily to each other, philosophers feel ignored by empiricists, experimenters resent the criticisms of rhetoricians, and teachers feel despised. It is for this reason, I submit, that part of the intellectual task of composition studies today is to understand and unify itself as a discipline" (Connors 1989, 235). These calls for unification came at precisely the same time that the various reading theories I detail in this chapter were making their way into professional journals, edited collections, and conference presentations, the very moment in which composition was working to define itself. The lack of unification that both of these scholars describe is represented in the fragmented program that *sought* to put reading front and center in composition (but ultimately did not), which, to return to Connors' metaphor, led to the movement's "fly[ing] apart like a dollar watch." Certainly, composition has always encouraged and fostered a range of theoretical and methodological approaches in part to honor the diversity of our students, and I am not suggesting that the compositionists discussed here should have limited themselves to a particular set of methodologies or theories. Rather, I am suggesting that those writing about reading might have more productively maintained a focus on reading rather than allowing their focus to become literature.

READING THE SCHOLARSHIP ON READING: LIMITS AND METHODS

The year 1980, the initial limit of this study, marks the publication in *College English* of English and Education scholar Charles Bazerman's groundbreaking article "A Relationship Between Reading and Writing: The Conversation Model," which challenges expressivist approaches from the period by "deemphasizing the writer's original voice, which has its source in an independent self" (Bazerman 1980, 657) and highlighting the more social aspects of writing. Instead of having students write "purely from their selves" (661), Bazerman encourages instructors to "consider each piece of writing as a contribution to an on-going written conversation" (657). Reading becomes crucial to this understanding of writing since "intelligent response begins *with accurate understanding of prior comments*" (658, emphasis in original). Bazerman's essay stands at the initial limit of this study because of the impact it had in composition and specifically on the reading movement. It has served as a touchstone for many other scholars who have sought to further develop its ideas in areas as diverse as ESL/ ELL pedagogies and writing across the curriculum pedagogies.

The year 1993 marks the year of the publication of Marguerite Helmers' collection of essays entitled *Intertexts: Reading Pedagogy in College Writing Classrooms*, the last collection of essays to explore the role of reading in composition instruction until the recent revival of interest in the subject. This is also the year that *College English* published the "Lindemann-Tate debate," wherein Erika Lindemann and Gary Tate revised for publication in *College English* their 1992 CCCC presentations on the place of literature in first-year composition. Although their stated topic was the place of *literature* (as opposed to *reading*), Lindemann seems just as invested in discussing reading, as opposed to the more narrow subject of reading literature. Helmers (2002, 8) believes that the debate and responses that followed "defined the terms that were to endure: literature and writing, not reading and writing." This debate marks the limit of this study because it is perhaps the most well-known scholarly discussion that exemplifies the tendency—even for compositionists—to conflate "reading" with "reading literature."

This chapter focuses on the most prevalent perspectives that emerged from my research and extensive reading of scholarship published between 1980 and 1993, but cannot be expected to represent all of the voices from the reading movement. It pays particular attention to the scholarship on reading that was published in the field's most widely circulating journals, such as *College Composition and Communication* and *College English*. This chapter also considers the collections and anthologies published during this period, and studies pieces that were reprinted in multiple publications and cited regularly in later pieces.

SLIPPAGES AND CONFLATIONS IN THE PERIOD'S SCHOLARSHIP

Time and time again in much of the scholarship from the 1980s and 1990s, we see a scholar who intends to write an essay on the place of reading in composition, but before long, the scholar "slips" and that term "reading" becomes "literature," often indicating the ideological and political investments of the scholar. At multiple, arbitrary moments in the piece the scholar may then return to the original term "reading." This seemingly innocuous slip has real consequences as the piece is no longer about the practice of reading, but about literature. In extreme cases of slippages, I use the term "conflation" to indicate that one term has become completely obscured and supplanted by another as in "reading" becoming supplanted by "literature" (with no return to the original term/subject). The sheer number of illustrations of this from the reading movement, a few of which I document below, makes it easier to understand why reading as a practice or process never became a focus of the field. Instead, the field became more interested in studying questions surrounding content, such as text selection and whether it is appropriate to read literature in composition classes. While the slippages and conflations I explore are one piece of the larger narrative of reading's failure to establish itself more solidly within the field, they nonetheless show how those scholars who drew largely on theories of reading from literary theory—as opposed to say from reading education—often deflected attention away from the topic of reading, the very topic they purported to be studying.

When "Reading" (verb) Becomes "Literature" and "Readings" (nouns)

It was common during this period to theorize the connections between reading and writing as a means to connect the fields of literature and composition. Discussions that located this as the ultimate goal of attending to reading-writing connections often conflated the terms "reading" and "literature" since just as composition brought writing to the table, literary studies brought literature (not reading). Focusing on two representative illustrations to draw out the implications of this trend, this section exemplifies how the politically-inflected reading movement really became about "*which kind of reading* gets to be theorized and practiced" (Salvatori 1996a, 185), and the answers given by scholars depended largely on what their specific investments were and how they imagined composition's place within their English departments and within English studies at large.

In Clifford and Schilb's 1985 essay, "Composition Theory and Literary Theory," published in the edited collection *Perspectives on Research and Scholarship in Composition,* the authors describe how the work of specific literary theorists and compositionists, including Ross Winterowd, Terry Eagleton, Wayne Booth, Nancy Comley, and Susan Miller, as well as current literary theory such as reader-response theory and post-structuralist theory, could be used to imagine and develop pedagogies that treat reading and writing as connected activities. Such work, they argued, could unify English.

In "Conversations with Texts: Reading in the Teaching of Composition," Salvatori criticizes Clifford and Schilb's essay on the grounds that it ultimately deflects attention away from the issue of reading since the place of reading in the teaching of composition "cannot be critically and reflexively engaged apart from the following interconnected questions:(1) Which theories of reading are better suited to teaching reading and writing as interconnected activities? (2) What is the theoretical justification for privileging that interconnectedness? (3) How can one teach that interconnectedness?" (Salvatori 1996b, 185). Salvatori's extensive engagement with these questions in the remainder of her essay underscores their importance. To her discussion I would add that Clifford and Schilb not only obscure the issue of reading in their neglect to answer these crucial questions, but obscure it through their constant slippage between the terms "reading" and "literature."

Clifford and Schilb (1985) open their essay by noting that "the last few years have witnessed several inspiring attempts

to fuse the teaching of writing with the teaching of literature. . . . Writing emerges as a process of discovery, enabling
students to construct knowledge rather than simply to regur-
gitate familiar truths or structural formulas. Literary study,
too, emerges as a dynamic event, one in which students can be
encouraged to draw on subjective insights as well as objective
perceptions as they gradually refine their sense of a text. The
act of writing and the act of reading literature can therefore
become for students mutually enhancing activities."

This excerpt, which sets up the focus of the piece, makes it
clear that the authors' shared interest lies in the relationship
between writing and what they interchangeably call "literary
study" and "reading literature." Shortly thereafter, though, the
terms of the discussion shift as Clifford and Schilb (1985) review
the contemporary scholarship. The examples they include seem
to be less about connections between literary study and writing
and more about connections between the processes of reading and writing. They discuss courses that drawing on reader-
response theory "intertwine the processes of reading and writing for students' productive engagement in both" (26). They
also describe the scholarship of Anthony Petrosky who "bases
his approach on the notion that reading and writing are both
composing acts, that understanding itself is a process of composing" (48). The authors slip again, though, in their summa-
tion of Petrosky's approach: "Combining literary theory and
composition theory, then, helps students understand themselves as readers and writers" (48). Notice how almost imperceptibly the authors move from a discussion of the acts of reading and writing to one about literary theory and composition
theory although Petrosky's scholarship is not invested in literary
theory. At the sentence-level, attention to reading is supplanted
by attention to literature.

This happens throughout the piece as Clifford and Schilb
review the scholarship of authors whose work revolves around
reading-writing connections, but then go on to shift the terms
and the context of this scholarship. Perhaps the last two head-
ings in their essay are most representative of these slippages

(as is the content these sections contain): "Unified Theories of Reading and Writing" and "What Kind of Literature?" While certainly there is room for these authors to address reading, writing, and literature in their essay, they conflate the discussion of literature with reading, leaving no room for a true discussion of the relationship between theories of reading and writing. In fact, the subject heading that suggests such a discussion will follow is misleading. The authors waste no time in the first section—"Unified Theories of Reading and Writing" moving to a different subject altogether, introducing this section in its first sentence as follows: "There are, however, even more ambitious possibilities for connections between the literature and composition components of the English curriculum" (58). Notice that "reading and writing" from the section heading have become "literature and composition." In the final section of their essay—"What Kind of Literature?" —Clifford and Schilb (1985) consider, "What kind of literature would most help students become better writers?" (65). The question that might have been asked is—What kind of reading practices would most help students become better writers? Although the subject heading suggests otherwise, this question also seems to interest the authors as they consider not just text selection, but how certain texts "promote the students' capacities for meaning making" (66). In the end, Clifford and Schilb prove less interested in reading and more interested in reading literature, to which their 2000 textbook *Making Literature Matter* attests. Still, this earlier piece illustrates the ease with which discussions from this period quickly shifted back and forth almost imperceptibly and almost always to the neglect of attention to reading as a practice.

The Lindemann-Tate debate also illustrates this problem. This "debate" describes presentations that Gary Tate and Erika Lindemann first presented in 1992 at the CCCC and then revised and published in *College English* in 1993 where additional scholars weighed in on the place of literature in first-year composition courses, both in the same issue and in later issues.[4] Although this debate may seem irrelevant to my project because of its overt investment in literature (i.e., not reading) and writing instruction, how it plays out is indicative of the ways in which efforts from this period to discuss reading as a practice (as Lindemann attempts to do) are ignored and overshadowed by investments in text selection.

Lindemann's position is that "we cannot usefully discuss the role of imaginative literature (however defined) in freshman English without first asking what the purpose of a first-year writing course is" and argues that the course "offers guided practice in reading and writing the discourses of the academy and the professions" (Lindemann 1993, 312) and as such there is no place for literature in it. "Such courses have as their subject matter," continues Lindemann, "the *processes* whereby writers and readers enter the conversations of the academy and begin to contribute to the making of knowledge. They focus not on nouns but on verbs: planning, drafting, revising, using data, evaluating sources, reading critically, interpreting evidence, solving problems in writing [and so on]" (313). Tate, as well as all of the respondents whose pieces are published in the issue, argue that imaginative literature does have a place in the composition classroom and completely ignore the distinction Lindemann makes between the teaching of literature in the first-year writing classroom and the teaching of reading. To Sharon Crowley's argument that the respondents' refusal to engage Lindemann's question about the point of the required first-year writing course "suggests that the point of composition matters somewhat less than the stature of literature" (Crowley 1998, 25), I would add that their refusal to recognize the distinction she makes between the teaching of reading (which she favors) and the teaching of literature (which she does not favor) is indicative, as well, of their content-centered ways of thinking that exclude attention to process and practice.

A Second Obstacle: Scholars' Differing Goals

Many scholars during this period saw the unification of the fields of composition and literature as a primary goal and they attempted to unify these fields through their scholarship, to which the title of Winifred Bryan Horner's 1983 edited collection of essays, *Composition and Literature: Bridging the Gap*, attests. Scholars who focus on reading-writing connections within this context are often calling for a restructuring of English around the processes of reading and writing as a means of uniting composition and literature. As discussed below, some scholars will describe the need for English to embrace broad paradigms based on discourse or textuality (instead of literature), for example, to combat the artificial separations between composition/writing and literature/reading. Others will argue for the unification of composition and literature based on a classical rhetorical model wherein rhetoric serves as a bridge between reading and writing. Others, still, were invested in reading-writing connections in order to develop effective writing pedagogies.

Attention to Reading-Writing Connections Means Better Writing Instruction

Not surprisingly, the group of scholars who theorized reading-writing connections with the goal of developing more effective writing pedagogies conceptualized the relationship of their scholarship in reading-writing connections to the teaching of writing. Both Berthoff and Salvatori attended to reading in order to help their students develop as writers. Berthoff's "double-entry" notebook makes visible the dialectical nature of reading and writing. On one side of the page students put "reading notes, direct quotations, observational notes, fragments, lists" while the other side records "notes about those notes," including "summaries, formulations, questions and queries and mumbles, editorial revisions, [and] comments on comments" (Berthoff 1982, 85). The facing pages," Berthoff notes, "are in dialogue with one another" and this method "assures that whatever is learned about reading is something learned about writing" (85–86).

Salvatori uses what she calls "the difficulty paper" in addition to the dialectical notebook to help her students realize that "understanding can emerge through an encounter with difficulty, and experiences of reading and writing will be enriched and enhanced if difficulty is addressed rather than ignored" (Salvatori and Donahue 2005, xxiv). This approach, like Berthoff's, is informed by her belief in the "theoretical and practical appropriateness of using reading as a means of teaching writing" (Salvatori 1996a, 182).

Haas and Flower's research was also driven by pedagogical goals. Describing their impetus for researching the reading process through their think-aloud protocol, they note that "a process we can't describe may be hard to teach. . . . If reading really is this constructive, rhetorical process," write Haas and Flower in the opening to their essay, "it may both demand that we rethink how we teach college students to read texts and suggest useful parallels between the act of reading and the more intensively studied process of writing" (Haas and Flower 1988, 167). Putting students at the center of their research (and sometimes using empirical methods), which had previously been the domain of K–12 Education specialists, compositionists made those in literary studies uneasy as their "less sophisticated" research seemed to threaten the literary-based research and theory that had long defined English departments.

Unlike Berthoff, Salvatori, Haas and Flower, and others in this camp, those compositionists whose work I study below are calling for the revival of rhetoric so that rhetoric can serve as a bridge between literature/reading and composition/writing. This, of course, proved another disconnect within the movement as the field could not come to a consensus on the significance of scholarship on reading-writing connections or how they would legitimize that very work. By linking composition to rhetoric and thus back to Ancient Greece and prominent figures such as Plato and Quintilian, scholars were able to claim a tradition for this field, a field that seemed new and questionable to many in English departments. Locating rhetoric as composition's progenitor was one way to validate its place within English departments.

Theorizing Connections between Reading
and Writing to Unify English

While in the 1950s Wayne Booth was committed to developing effective pedagogies that capitalized on reading-writing connections, his investments expanded in the 1980s to include theorizing new disciplinary structures that represent the relationship between the work of literature and composition. Rhetoric guides his call for the restructuring of English and serves as the bridge that connects composition and literature. In his essay "LITCOMP," Booth (1983, 79) describes the aptly named course as asking students "not just to study the texts but to do something like the text, to practice the rhetoric the texts exhibit, and to reflect . . . on that practice." The development and teaching of courses that focus on "critical capacities," including the "capacity to shape reality with words" (64) is Booth's way of counteracting the "increasingly sharp divisions" within English. As he laments the reasons for these divisions he remarks that "only the most inviting of programs can offer any hope of reversing those trends" (57). The course he describes and others like it, argues Booth, offer an opportunity to do just that, to "remake ourselves and our circumstances," to close what he refers to as "The Great Widening Gap." "We are the best-trained rhetoricians in the country," writes Booth, and "unless that training has been only in how to write passable 'literary criticism,' we ought to be able, working together, to discover ways of remaking our profession" (80).

Also committed to restructuring English, Nancy Comley and Robert Scholes were interested in not only "deconstructing the system of oppositions that supports the split between literature and composition" but showing what can be done "in daily academic lives to dismantle the practices in which we are enmeshed" and replace them with better ones (Comley and Scholes 1983, 101). One of the principal ways of doing so, according to Comley and Scholes, is to get past the tendency to focus on literature and to focus more broadly, instead, on textuality and the production and consumption of it. Although they do not use the term "rhetoric" to describe their approach it seems fair to do so. The relevance of rhetoric to their project becomes even more pronounced in their co-authored (with Gregory Ulmer) textbook volume entitled *Text-Book* that challenges the split between literary and non-literary texts in order to focus on rhetorical aspects of all writing. Moreover, while their co-authored work doesn't invoke rhetoric outright, Scholes' later work, *The Rise and Fall of English,* seems to develop the theory on which *Text-Book,* his influential *Textual Power,* as well as his earlier work with Comley is founded as he argues for "a discipline based on rhetoric and the teaching of reading and writing over a broad range of texts" (Scholes 1999, 179). "The principal object" of the discipline he imagines is "textuality, rather than literature" (147). As Comley and Scholes note in their co-authored essay, no matter whether the class is one in "composition" or in "literature," English faculty should focus on a "writing approach to literary texts, in which students write in the forms they are reading or use such texts as intertexts for writing in other forms" in order to "improve their ability to write in all forms of discourse and improve their ability to read and interpret texts" (Comley and Scholes 1983, 108). Attending to reading and writing as connected practices through the concepts of rhetoric, textuality, and discourse, Comely and Scholes, like Booth, imagine that curricular change has the power to bridge the gaps within the system of oppositions that characterized (and continue to characterize English) at the time.

Other scholars who sought to connect literature and composition through rhetoric were more concerned with the role history might play in the restructuring of English. James Murphy, for example, argued in his essay "Rhetorical History as a Guide to the Salvation of American Reading and Writing: A Plan for Curricular Courage" that we "must learn our own history" and "understand the rhetorical tradition itself" since in the Western cultural tradition, until this century, reading and writing were not separated, but treated "as complementary modes of an integrated whole" (Murphy 1982, 7). Although the title of his piece seems to promise the inclusion of some ideas for curricular change, unlike Booth and Scholes and Comely, Murphy stops short of doing so, yet he anticipates this work: "What is needed, first of all, is the historical sense to realize that this separation of writing from reading was indeed brought about in America by conscious choice. . . . Then, having identified what has got us into the current mess, we can decide how to make the reintegration of reading and writing that we abandoned earlier in this century" (8). Murphy does not go on to describe what this reintegration might look like. This proved a sticking point for those who were invested in studying reading-writing connections in order to develop more effective writing pedagogies. Although her comments are not directed at Murphy or any scholar in particular, Salvatori has addressed the importance of developing and enacting theoretical developments within composition through pedagogical interventions. These theories, she claims, do not "automatically and necessarily lead to their own rigorous enactment" (Salvatori 1996a, 186). Speaking specifically to the relationship between reading and writing, Salvatori notes that "to foreground and to teach—rather than just to understand—that interconnectedness [between reading and writing] is a highly constructed, unnatural and obtrusive activity" (187). That is to say that it takes deliberate and relentless attention to develop and sustain a pedagogy based on this connectedness. However, what Salvatori fails to address is that not everyone working on reading-writing connections was doing so to improve writing instruction. To fault these compositionists for not following through with the development of new pedagogies is to assume a shared set of motivations and goals, which is to ignore the conflicts at the time, in this case between research and pedagogy.

BEYOND THE DISSONANCES: TRACING THE CONNECTIONS IN THE SCHOLARSHIP FROM THE 1980S AND 1990S

Despite the ideological, political, and disciplinary forces that informed the dissonances detailed in the first section of this chapter, the scholarship from this period names and develops a series of foundational concepts and ideas about reading that seem worth recovering in order to productively re-introduce reading into the field.

First, whether privileging cognitive psychology, literary, rhetorical, or educational theory, scholars from this period were working on theorizing a type of reading that would stand in opposition to reading that has been characterized by Mariolina Salvatori as "enervated" and "atrophied": "A reading immobilized within textbooks and reduced therein to sets of disparate simplifying practices that, separated from the various theories that motivate them, turn into meaningless and arbitrary *exercises*: reading for *the main idea*, for *plot*, for *argument*, for *point of view*, for *meaning*, for *message*—interchangeably and without knowing why. Or reading texts as inscrutable and unquestionable 'models' of style or rhetorical strategies. Or as 'blueprints' for linguistic theories, political programmes, or philosophies of language" (Salvatori 1996a, 184, emphasis in original). In place of this "atrophied" way of reading, these scholars located reading as writing's counterpart in the construction of meaning. Whether (implicitly or explicitly) drawing on Louise Rosenblatt's notion of the transaction between reader and text, Frank Smith's contention that reading "is an aspect of thinking and learning" (xii), Berthoff's (1982) conception of reading as "a way of coming to know, of learning to learn," or Brower and Poirier's (1962) "reading in slow motion," the scholars writing about reading in the 1980s and 1990s are united by their emphasis on reading as an active, dynamic practice of constructing meaning rather than a simple practice of decoding. This way of understanding reading informs (albeit largely implicitly) scholarship in literary studies and composition today. As Patricia Harkin points out, this conception of reading is "simply assumed in every aspect of our work. . . . Thoroughly normalized, it has more or less ceased to be exciting." She explains further, "Many people have never known a time in the academy when it has not been normal to accept this proposition without demur. But since it was not always thus, it is important . . . for older folks to remember and younger folks to imagine how amazing it was to hear it for the first time. Readers make meaning: readers—and not only authors—engage in an active process of production-in-use in which texts of all kinds—stories, poems, plays, buildings, films, TV ads, clothes, body piercings—are received by their audiences not as a repository of stable meaning but as an invitation to make it" (Harkin 2005, 413). As discussed in the previous chapter, composition embraced reader-response theory's focus on the reader as composer of meaning and reading as the very act of composing.

A second, noteworthy concept that emerges from the scholarship on reading from the 1980s and 1990s is that reading and writing, although not exactly the same process, are connected processes. While this point in and of itself does not seem particularly groundbreaking (although it was groundbreaking in ways that the previous chapter suggests), the scholarship produced during this time on reading and reading-writing connections established that just as writing need not only to be taught, but also theorized, so did reading. This notion is, of course, related to the point above that because reading is such a dynamic process it cannot be defined as merely decoding. Instead, it must be theorized, investigated, and explored so that the teaching of reading is theoretically grounded. The very notion that reading—not just at the lower levels (as had been done for years in K–12 education)—needed to be theorized is a foundational idea upon which all of this scholarship depends.

A third, significant point that these scholars make might be thought of as the product of the first and second points, namely that reading is a complex practice. Prior to this moment, as detailed in the previous chapter, reading was largely defined in rather simplistic terms that associated it with elocution and decoding. As Salvatori and Donahue (2012, 203) describe, reading "is a complex term that signifies a range of ideas, practices, assumptions, and identities. The recognition of its complexity only increases when it is understood that different theories of reading lead to different approaches to the reading of texts (especially student texts) in addition to the teaching of writing." This point about the complexity of reading is crucial to keep in mind as we reanimate discussions of reading in composition.

While it is unlikely that compositionists will return to thinking about reading as decoding, we do not want to forget that even as we acknowledge the complexity of the act of reading we must also remain aware that precisely because "different theories of reading lead to different approaches to the reading of texts," none of these approaches is neutral, but, instead, each reflects the theory upon which each depends.

A related point worth underscoring is the emphasis these scholars place on the approaches themselves, on *how* texts mean rather than *what* they mean. Whether a scholar advocates close reading, largely considered a text-centered approach, or one of the reader-centered approaches that falls under the reader-response umbrella, the scholarship from the 1980s and 1990s makes this important distinction visible, and clearly values the *how* as scholars approach this question from a multitude of perspectives. Moreover, as the previous chapter details, reading became a subject of inquiry at this time precisely because the juxtaposition of these two literary-theoretical-pedagogical formations suggested that the practice of reading was not as simple as previously thought. In fact, one way to begin to answer the question of why the subject of reading is currently experiencing a revival in composition is to consider the ways in which the contemporary need to read across media and devices is exposing— once again—the complexity of reading, just as reader-response theory demonstrated that the act of reading is not reducible to "the text itself." The distinction between text-centered and reader-centered approaches bears keeping in mind as compositionists return to theorizing reading's place in the field of composition and the composition classroom.

The final common element across the scholarship from the 1980s and 1990s that I will describe is perhaps the subtlest because among those scholars mentioned in this chapter, only Haas and Flower overtly studied reading by focusing on cognition. Although other scholars who also did so are not mentioned in this chapter, this was a common approach during this era with many essays on the relationship between reading and cognition appearing in Ann M. Penrose and Barbara M. Sitko's edited collection *Hearing Ourselves Think* (Penrose and Sitko 1993). Taking the complexity of the act of reading seriously, this scholarship studies the brain's role in that complexity. Even when scholars from this period do not explicitly align themselves with or use the terminology from cognitive or educational psychology, they acknowledge the importance of studying and finding various ways to actively engage the brain in order to read in sophisticated ways. For example, you will recall that Berthoff and Salvatori and Donahue have developed assignments such as the difficulty paper and the double- and triple-entry notebook that ask students to reflexively self-monitor, to re-*cognize* and reflect on their ways of reading. Although not empirically studying reading practices within a cognitive framework, these scholars, nonetheless, drew extensively on the cognitive aspects of reading as they formulated their pedagogies. This emphasis on cognition and particularly on metacognition—on thinking about one's own thinking—becomes a crucial foundation for the "mindful reading" framework I will advocate in later chapters.

A CLOSER LOOK AT A WIDELY-CIRCULATING COMPOSITION READER THAT FOREGROUNDS READING-WRITING CONNECTIONS: *WAYS OF READING: AN ANTHOLOGY FOR WRITERS*

Perhaps the most compelling representation of how the elements I acknowledged just above coalesced into a coherent program comes in the form of Bartholomae and Petrosky's composition reader *Ways of Reading.*[5] Despite the field's changing investments since the 1980s and its lack of interest in the production of scholarship on reading, *Ways of Reading*, first published in 1987 and now in its tenth edition (Bartholomae, Petrosky, and Waite 2014), did emerge from this period and has experienced continued success. I conclude this chapter by considering *Ways of Reading*, which is situated as both an apparent anomaly in a field that has neglected reading for decades, as well as a text that embodies what we might recover from the scholarship produced on reading in the 1980s and 1990s.

When it was published in 1987, *Ways of Reading* was imagined by its editor Chuck Christensen at Bedford/St. Martin's as a reader that would compete with the *Norton Reader*. Bartholomae (2011) has said that he and Petrosky "put together what made sense to [them] and what drew on [their] teaching," which had very little in common with the *Norton Reader*. Even from the first edition, *Ways of Reading* challenges the oppositions between so-called literature and non-literature or literature and nonfiction upon which other contemporary readers (and English as a discipline) depended. "We realize that we are ignoring traditional distinctions between fiction and nonfiction," write Bartholomae and Petrosky (1987, viii) in the preface to the first edition, "but we are not sure that these are key distinctions in a course that presents reading as an action to be completed by writing." In fact, as they also point out in the preface, the selections are better understood not in terms of their genres, but as "selections that invite students to be active readers and to take responsibility for their acts of interpretation" (iv).

While Bartholomae and Petrosky were not interested in perpetuating the traditional distinctions that characterize other readers from the time, they were committed to distinguishing their ways of understanding and teaching reading from the ways reading was more commonly taught. From the first paragraph of the preface wherein they note that their students were able to "read sentences" and "carry out many of the versions of reading required for their education—skimming textbooks, cramming for tests, strip-mining books for term papers" (iii)—Bartholomae and Petrosky (1987) set the context within which they will describe their pedagogy and the forms of reading that it opposes. Throughout the preface to the first edition, this prerogative emerges as they describe their approach in contrast to those that simply ask students to "get the point" by reading "short set-pieces" (iv). Bartholomae and Petrosky (1987) describe these more commonly anthologized pieces: "These can be read in a single sitting; they make arguments that can be easily paraphrased; they solve all the problems they raise; they wrap up Life and put it into a box; and so they turn reading into an act of appreciation, where the most that seems to be required is a nod of the head. And they suggest that a writer's job is to do just that, to write a piece that is similarly tight and neat and self-contained" (iv). While Bartholomae and Petrosky concede that the type of reading these selections foster has its place, they imagined themselves as working against the assumptions that informed this approach, including the degree of difficulty students could handle and what types of practices they could be expected to engage in as they read and write. Bartholomae and Petrosky's approach was not without its detractors and at the time that they taught Basic Reading and Writing at the University of Pittsburgh, a course based on their theories of reading and writing detailed in *Ways of Reading*, they had to defend themselves and their pedagogy before the Dean, as well as before the College of Arts and Sciences council. Bartholomae (2005) has described this uphill battle: "We were actually at war with the reading researchers and reading specialists on our own campus, who wanted to have a course that was really a study skills course" (364). Bartholomae and Petrosky justified their approach through the work of literary critic Frank Kermode and English education scholar Frank Smith who gave them "a way of imagining reading as, in a sense, a compositional activity" (364). With this understanding of reading in mind, they included selections that challenged attempts to simply find information or locate an author's purpose (Bartholomae and Petrosky 1987, 1), selections that "require more attention than an easy summary or a quick reduction to main ideas" (9). Bartholomae and Petrosky describe the type of reading their pedagogy depends upon as "a social interaction" wherein students speak in the writer's place, "sometimes for them, doing their work, continuing their projects" (1). This reading is "strong, aggressive, [and] labor-intensive" (5) and is connected to writing and thinking. Drawing on one of the most widely circulating terms from this period, Bartholomae and Petrosky (1987) describe their type of reading as "critical reading," as they note that "strong readers often read critically, weighing, for example, an author's claims and interpretations against evidence—evidence provided by the author in the text, evidence drawn from other sources, or the evidence that is assumed to be part of a reader's own knowledge and experience" (11). This type of reading manifests itself in assignments that ask students to reread each piece to notice relationships among ideas, as well as key terms and concepts presented in these long, difficult pieces. Assignments also ask students to test, measure, and extend authors' arguments. Reading is discussed throughout the assignments, as well as in the introductory materials, as complementary to writing—and sometimes even as indistinguishable from it: "The connection between reading and writing can be seen as almost a literal one, since the best way you can show your reading of a rich and dense essay . . . is by writing down your thoughts, placing one idea against another, commenting on what you've done, taking examples into account, looking back at where you began, perhaps changing your mind, and moving on" (11).

Anyone familiar with the most recent editions of *Ways of Reading* will recognize this approach and these types of assignments as they have not changed much since the first edition. The text's apparatus that explains its pedagogy and purpose in the tenth edition of *Ways of Reading* is remarkably similar to that of its first incarnation, particularly in terms of how it defines reading and how it enacts this pedagogy through its selections and assignment sequences. The tenth edition, and those that come before it, continue to emphasize critical reading, the importance of rereading, as well as reading with and against the grain. This, of course, challenges my contention that attention to reading has waned considerably since the 1990s. After all, since its fourth edition, *Ways of Reading* has been a market-leader and continues to be used at colleges and universities across the country. How is it that a composition textbook whose pedagogy depends upon reading-writing connections has been so successful in a field that has largely neglected reading as a topic that demands inquiry? It seems that the textbook's focus on reading, though, isn't necessarily responsible for its success or used as a selling point by its marketers. In an email correspondence, David Bartholomae (2011) describes the success of *Ways of Reading* as tied to how it makes instructors feel about their work in the composition classroom: "[People] may follow this wave or that, but they come back to something that gives them the opportunity to be proud of their work." In fact, the importance of this sense of pride to the textbook's success pervades the positive feedback that Bartholomae and Petrosky, as well as the publisher have received. "When we hear from students and teachers, it's always the same thing," explains Bartholomae. "The book/the course took me seriously and gave me work to be proud of." In an interview conducted by Jeffrey J. Williams with the *Minnesota Review* Bartholomae said something similar: "The pleasure of the textbook is hearing from people for whom it's been an important experience, teachers and students, saying something like, 'The book took me seriously as a thinking person.' I refer to students as intellectuals, and people laugh at that, but I'm not being ironic. They're trying on the role of the intellectual, and we help them do that by forms of engagement we arrange." (Bartholomae 2007)

Representatives from Bedford/St. Martin's who market the book use this feedback as a selling point. Rather than covering over or downplaying the difficulty (both from a teacher's and student's perspective) of *Ways of Reading*, they explain to instructors the importance of setting the bar high through difficult readings and new approaches to reading. In other words, they characterize the approach of *Ways of Reading* as one that creates a space for teachers and students to do intellectually rigorous work together. Many instructors have reported to Bedford/St. Martin's that once they have used *Ways of Reading* there is no going back to easily digestible texts.

Based on the feedback from those who use *Ways of Reading*, it would seem that its draw has more to do with its overall conception as a textbook that takes instructors seriously in their pursuits and that allows students to participate in and extend intellectual projects that respected scholars such as Michel Foucault, Edward Said, and Adrienne Rich have begun. Although its focus on reading is certainly part of that mission, that focus does not seem to account for its success and continued use by instructors. Neither is its emphasis on reading something that its publisher underscores or uses as a means to market the textbook. Still, as a market-leader for decades now, *Ways of Reading* exemplifies the success of a project that frames the practice of reading as something other than remedial, a goal that scholars—no matter their perspective—in the 1980s and 1990s were working toward. Building a pedagogy based on some of the central concepts that emerged from reading scholarship in the 1980s, including those discussed above, *Ways of Reading* directly and consistently challenges theories and pedagogies of reading that reduce reading to a mechanical, simplistic, over-determined practice.

Remaining cognizant of how reading has a history of being reduced to a practice of little more than decoding, a conception that *Ways of Reading* and the scholars in the 1980s and 1990s rejected, is important as we find ways to reanimate discussions about reading in composition for they have the potential to help us understand the current place of reading in composition. Having outlined what may have led to the current situation wherein first-year writing instructors recognize the importance of teaching reading alongside writing, but who have not been prepared to do so because reading has been largely neglected by the field for the past two decades, the following chapter returns to my study of first-year writing instruction in order to explore how these historical antecedents might productively influence and address the goals these instructors shared in their surveys and interviews. To return to the point made by David Jolliffe, with which this chapter began: "Because the topic of reading lies outside the critical discourse of composition studies" instructors do "not have access to ample resources to help them think about a model of active constructive reading in the courses or about strategies for putting that model into play" (Jolliffe 2007, 478). The remainder of this book seeks to provide those very resources and strategies.

NOTES

1. *Reader* has since expanded its focus and extended its reach as it passed from Michigan Tech to Paul Kameen at the University of Pittsburgh and ultimately to Lafayette College where Patricia Donahue currently edits the journal.

2. As I note in the introduction, this phrase does not do justice to the diversity of perspectives that characterize the scholarship from the period, but it will need to suffice as shorthand for the corpus of scholarship produced at this time.

3. The shift in thinking that the "social turn" refers to was characterized by attention to writing's social dimensions and the rise in popularity of practical applications such as peer editing, peer tutoring, and co-authoring. This paradigm removed the writer from isolation, situating her, instead, as a social being affected by cultural, political, and social forces. In "Taking the Social Turn: Teaching Writing Post-Process," the review essay responsible for introducing the term "post-process" to the field, John Trimbur (1994, 109) describes this turn as characterized by a representation of "literacy as an ideological arena and composing as a cultural activity by which writers position and reposition themselves in relation to their own and others' subjectivities, discourse practices, and institutions." The "post" in "post process" is intended to indicate a shift from considering process as the framework for understanding writing to considering the social aspects of writing, including those political and cultural forces. For an exploration of how conceptions of writing have evolved as they have (and in the sequence they have) within composition studies see Martin Nystrand's "Where Did Composition Studies Come From?: An Intellectual History." At this particular time of the "social turn," when literacy was (first) thought of as an "ideological arena," a dominant form of reading that emerged was ideological critique and reading that was beginning to be understood as an ideologically-bound activity in and of itself.

4. The debate was revisited in 1995 in *College English* and additional scholars weighed in on the place of literature in composition.

5. For an in-depth discussion of how five "popular" contemporary composition readers attend to reading see Debrah Huffman's (2010) "Towards Modes of Reading in Composition." Although there is not sufficient space in this manuscript to address how textbooks contribute to composition's vexed relationship to reading, it is a subject worth studying as evidenced by Huffman's compelling piece.

5

TRANSFER OF LEARNING SCHOLARSHIP AND READING INSTRUCTION IN FIRST-YEAR COMPOSITION

The study detailed in Chapter 2, which focuses primarily on how instructors attend to reading in their composition classes (and how students experience these connections), found that forty-eight percent (n = 48) of instructors teach what they call "rhetorical reading" and/or "rhetorical analysis." They employ this approach as a means to reach two primary goals: (1) to connect the practices of reading and writing, and (2) to prepare students to read effectively in other and future courses. These instructors value rhetorical reading because it potentially combats students' default way of "reading for information" and compels them to pay attention to other elements that give them insight into how a text "is working" (Erma 2012). As detailed in that chapter, the data collected from both the instructor-driven and student-driven aspects of the survey suggest that rhetorical reading does allow instructors to effectively connect the processes of reading and writing. To what extent, though, does this focus on rhetorical reading meet instructors' second goal, namely to prepare their students to read effectively in other classes? I look to scholarship and research from the fields of educational and cognitive psychology for a better understanding of how knowledge and learning transfer from one context to another. This exploration lays the foundation for the following chapter which, drawing on this scholarship and research, introduces a theory of reading and details how to teach and enact it.

DOI: 10.7330/9780874219609.c005

RESEARCH ON THE TRANSFER OF LEARNING AND KNOWLEDGE

Despite instructors' investment in effectively preparing students to read in courses beyond their own, only one instructor noted that she teaches rhetorical reading with an eye toward other contexts. She described giving students "a transferable rhetorical lens" that includes "core questions/approaches for different kinds of texts" (Deena 2012). None of the other instructors detailed reading pedagogies that foreground to students how rhetorical reading is useful beyond first-year composition. One might wonder—as do these astute instructors—if their students who are writing their own "modest proposals," for example, will transfer anything they learn from completing that assignment into future classes. We cannot answer this question definitively, but following the lead of Haas and Flower, as well as many other scholars during the 1980s and 1990s, I look to scholars within the fields of educational and cognitive psychology. I take this interdisciplinary approach to make use of research on how knowledge transfers from one context to another in order to consider if and how teaching students to rhetorically read transfers to other contexts.

For close to three decades, David Perkins and Gavriel Salomon, two educational psychologists, have been studying transfer within the context of educational sites. In "Transfer of Learning," which provides an overview of the findings from their scholarship on transfer, Perkins and Salomon (1992) note that "the transfer of learning occurs when learning in one context or with one set of materials impacts on performance in another context or with other related materials" (Perkins and Salomon 1992, n.p.). King Beach, who takes a social-cultural approach, expands Perkins and Salomon's notion of transfer to include not just individual, task-based applications from one context to the next, but the social contexts that inform these experiences. In fact, he rejects the term "transfer" because it does not do justice to the multiple facets and dynamics of the process. Beach, instead, prefers the term "generalize" and discusses how people generalize from one context to the next. This term encompasses the more commonplace notion of transfer wherein an individual applies knowledge from one context to another, but also emphasizes that the individual is always part of a larger social organization as is the activity in which she is engaging. Generalizing for Beach, who considers sites of learning, as well as other activities, is characterized by the "continuity and transformation of knowledge, skill, and identity across various forms of social organization" and is marked by "interrelated processes rather than a single general procedure" (Beach 1999, 112). He describes forms of generalization as "not located within the developing individual, nor can they simply be reduced to changes in social activities. Rather, these forms of generalization are located in the changing relation between persons and activities" (113). Beach's examples are instructive in demonstrating how his theory expands Perkins and Salomon's (and other common) depictions of transfer:

> Experiences such as learning algebra after years of studying arithmetic, becoming a machinist, founding a community organization, teaching one's firstborn to walk, an elementary school class writing a letter to a local newspaper, collaborating with NASA scientists on a classroom project via the Internet, making the transition from student to teacher, and negotiating one's identity as an African American between home and the school are all potential examples of . . . generalization. Each of these experiences can involve transformation, the construction of new knowledge, identities, ways of knowing, and new positionings of oneself in the world. They are consequential for the individual and are developmental in nature, located in the changing relations between individuals and social activities. (113)

As we consider Beach's approach to "transfer," it is useful to pay attention to his use of the words "transformation," "constructions," and "positionings" because these suggest his investment in the dynamics of generalizing, which are seemingly always in motion as generalizing affects and is simultaneously affected by the individual and the activity. Beach's more dynamic understanding of "transfer" is useful as a means to exposing the different forces at play when a student moves from one context to another. Moreover, it reminds us that it is not simply the context that is changing, but that the student, and the relationship that the student has to the context is in flux. In other words, nothing about this process is static.

Although they work from different theoretical foundations, Perkins, Salomon and Beach agree that participants must *recognize* the abstract or general principles inherent in one activity (e.g., solving a mathematical equation) in order to "transfer" that knowledge into a future context (e.g., solving a rhetorical problem). While some of this work is the responsibility of the participant, in the case of transfer within educational contexts, instructors can teach to facilitate transfer. They can, in other words, teach their students how to deliberately and consistently recognize the general principles inherent in any given activity or context that might be of use in other or future contexts and activities. As Richard E. Mayer and Merlin C. Wittrock describe in "Problem-Solving Transfer," "schools are not able to teach students everything they will need to know, but rather must equip students with the ability to transfer. . . . Transfer is a pervasive characteristic of human cognition: New learning is always dependent on previous learning" (Mayer and Wittrock 1996, 49).

Metacognition—literally thinking about thinking—is the hinge upon which transfer depends. (Too) simply put, transfer has the potential to occur when students *recognize* and *generalize* something in one (perhaps a previous) course in order to allow for application in a different course. Those acts of recognition and generalization are crucial or transfer cannot occur.

Transfer of learning scholars have developed a range of distinctions among types of transfer, which include high road and low road transfer; positive and negative transfer; near and far transfer; and forward reaching and backward reaching transfer. It is worth noting that these types of transfer—even those that seem to oppose each other—often actually overlap and complement each other in practice. Perkins and Salomon explain that low road transfer (sometimes called near transfer) "happens when stimulus conditions in the transfer context are sufficiently similar to those in a prior context of learning to trigger well-developed semi-automatic responses" while high road transfer (sometimes called far transfer) "depends on mindful abstraction from the context of learning or application and a deliberate search for connections" (Perkins and Salomon 1992, sec. 5). Forward-reaching transfer depends upon the initial situation serving as the impetus for anticipating future uses or applications while backward-reaching transfer happens when the participant thinks back to a previous situation in order to make relevant connections. While low road transfer happens often enough, high road transfer is difficult to achieve. High road transfer has the potential "to bridge between contexts remote from one another . . . it requires the effort of deliberate abstraction and connection making and the ingenuity to make the abstractions and discover the connections" (Perkins and Salomon 1988, 27). Although none of the instructors I spoke to specified the type of transfer they hoped to encourage through their teaching, they seemed committed, in particular (as I would argue many teaching general education courses are), to facilitating high-road, both forward- and backward-facing transfer since this form of transfer depends upon making connections across a range of disciplines both in the moment and later in one's academic career. According to transfer of learning scholars, though, these are the most difficult forms of transfer to facilitate because they depend upon the transfer of learning between contexts that appear to be very different from one another.[1]

The difficulty of teaching for transfer has not escaped the instructors I surveyed and interviewed as the majority wondered whether what they teach their students about reading will transfer beyond first-year composition. We might conclude that unless instructors help students generalize the abstract principles present in the modeling and rhetorical reading exercises in which they ask students to engage, these remain singular activities tied to the specific course, instructor, and assignment. With the exception of the one instructor who describes her teaching of a "transferable rhetorical lens," mentioned previously; two instructors who teach students how to "self-monitor" their comprehension abilities as they read; and a final instructor who mentioned the importance of helping students develop metacognitive skills through "difficulty papers" and other assignments, the majority of instructors with whom I spoke do not seem to be teaching rhetorical reading within the necessary metacognitive framework thought to produce these connections. Thus, their teaching of reading may not be promoting high-road or far transfer. Certainly these instructors encourage low road or near transfer as they support their students' rhetorical reading of models and then the use of those rhetorical moves in students' own essays. But, the instructors do not seem to generalize rhetorical reading in such a way that students recognize its relationship to reading they will complete in other classes.

Take again, for example, Darla, the instructor who uses Swift's "A Modest Proposal" in order to model for students this particular genre so that students can then compose their own modest proposals. Darla, like many other instructors with whom I spoke, teaches rhetorical reading through the use of model texts and does so in order to explicitly teach particular genres. Students rhetorically read these texts in order to locate the elements of a particular genre, which they are then expected to imitate in their writing. Certainly these instructors are connecting the processes of reading and writing, which is crucial to motivating students to complete the reading in a writing course, but the way in which they are doing so might more productively facilitate transfer if they were to focus more on cultivating students' *awareness* of the relationship between genres and reading practices. As research in educational psychology and transfer of learning studies indicates, that very *awareness* is the transferable element. The genre of "the modest proposal" (and, for that matter, many genres and their associated conventions that might be taught) has very limited relevance beyond the context of that first-year composition class. Taught apart from a metacognitive framework that fosters the recognition and generalization of the transferrable element, namely awareness (and not the genre per se), the same might be said about rhetorical reading. In other words, rhetorical reading as a specific practice used in English studies may not be relevant across contexts, but the awareness of its existence and its potential uses *are* relevant.

It is not just rhetorical reading that proves problematic, but *all* reading approaches that are taught apart from a metacognitive framework intended to promote transfer. David Smit notes in the *End of Composition Studies* that "writing teachers get what they teach for, instruction in particular kinds of knowledge and skill and not broad-based writing ability. If we want to promote the transfer of certain kinds of writing abilities from one class to another or one context to another, then we are going to have to find the means to institutionalize instruction in the similarities between the way writing is done in a variety of contexts" (Smit 2004, 119–120). We might say the same about reading.

The many insightful instructors I spoke to, like Marshall, who worry about "how well [students' rhetorical analysis skills] sink in and transfer beyond [his] course" challenge the contention that educators believe that "transfer takes care of itself" (Perkins and Salomon 1988, 23). Still, they, along with other educators face a major challenge, for as Smit laments, "Overwhelmingly, the evidence suggests that learners do not necessarily transfer the kinds of knowledge and skills they have learned previously to new tasks" (Smit 2004, 119). It would seem to follow, then, that if we want to help first-year composition instructors reach their goal of supporting students' development of rhetorical reading approaches that will transfer into other courses we need to ask questions about what reading instruction looks like in relation to what we know about how learning and knowledge travel from one context to the next. Based on what we know from psychology about the importance of encouraging generalization in order to promote transfer, it would follow that unless the instructors I spoke with are teaching rhetorical reading within this context then transfer is less likely to occur. One can only hypothesize about the degree to which reading knowledge transfers because the research emerging from composition on learning transfer is relatively slow to come.[2] Moreover, even the most recent, exciting set of essays written by compositionists on transfer, published in *Composition Forum*'s (fall 2012) special issue on "Writing and Transfer" focus exclusively on the transfer of writing—not reading—knowledge.[3]

Still, these and earlier essays on the transfer of writing "skills" might provide useful resources for thinking about the transfer of reading. The articles throughout *Composition Forum*'s special issue consistently refer to what are becoming a few seminal pieces in composition on the topic of transfer. These include three articles, all published in *WPA* in 2007, as well as Anne Beaufort's 2007 book *College Writing and Beyond,* detailing a longitudinal case study of a student's attempt to transfer the writing skills he learned in first-year composition. Gerald Nelms and Rhonda Leathers Dively's article "Perceived Roadblocks to Transferring Knowledge from First-Year Composition to Writing-Intensive Major Courses: A Pilot Study" examines a study they conducted at their university, Southern Illinois University Carbondale, in order to determine "what specific concepts, strategies, and skills are reportedly being emphasized and practiced in . . . English 101 and 102 [that] seem to transfer to the College of Applied Science's writing-intensive courses" (Nelms and Dively 2007, 219). Elizabeth Wardle's "Understanding 'Transfer' from FYC: Preliminary Results of a Longitudinal Study" encourages the teaching of generalization in first-year composition classes and Linda S. Bergman and Janet Zepernick's "Disciplinarity and Transference: Students' Perceptions of Learning to Write," addresses the subject of transfer primarily from students' perspectives. Since 2007, at least two transfer-centered studies have been supported by WPA Research grants, "The Case for Authentic Transfer: A Longitudinal Study of Writing-Skills Transfer" and "Rethinking Transfer, Renewing Pedagogy: Knowledge Transfer Research and Its Implications for Revising FYC," although their results are not yet published.

In addition to these forthcoming results, Elon University has developed a multi-year research seminar to explore how issues of transfer affect the teaching of writing. The "Elon Research Seminar on Critical Transitions: Writing and the Question of Transfer" is a multi-institutional seminar that features forty participants from across four continents. The first meeting was held in the summer of 2011 and these scholars in rhetoric and composition met in North Carolina "to discuss the challenges around the concept of transfer and the future of transfer research. Participants spent six days collaborating about the critical transitions for transfer, including first-year composition to general education, the major to the workplace, the writing center to writing sites" (Taczak 2012). Interviews with these participants are published in *Composition Forum*'s special issue on "Writing and Transfer," mentioned above, and their articles, which appear in this issue, guest-edited by Elizabeth Wardle, often call for additional research on if and how writing "skills" transfer, as do Nelms and Dively in their essay.

This chapter and the following answer Nelms and Dively's (2007, 230) call for making the "facilita[tion] of the transfer of composition knowledge a priority of our discipline," but perhaps not in the way these scholars anticipated since the focus is on reading—not writing—as an act of composition. I hypothesize that we can better promote the transfer of reading knowledge by creating composition courses that encourage the development of metacognitive practices that encourage students to generalize by abstracting the general principles of the reading practices they are taught. In the following chapter, I describe in more detail what I call a *mindful reading* framework within which to teach reading. Mindful reading is best understood *not* as yet another way of reading, but a *framework* for teaching the range of ways of reading (e.g., rhetorical reading, critical reading, close reading) that are currently valued in our field so that students can create knowledge *about* reading and *about* themselves as readers, knowledge that they can bring with them into other courses.

That last sentence is likely to raise some criticism because it brings to the fore one of the foundational assumptions upon which this chapter depends, namely that reading is a generalizable skill. This characterization of writing has long been contested in composition particularly by scholars like Patricia Bizzell and Kenneth Bruffee who have spent time studying "discourse communities." These scholars contend that social context heavily influences and governs one's writing. They focus on the local conventions of these contexts rather than considering similarities that may exist across contexts. The mindful reading framework does not deny that reading, like writing, is bound to communities of social practice and particular contexts. In fact, teaching reading within this framework emphasizes this point since instructors are responsible for helping students recognize, understand, and anticipate their relationship to reading in a range of contexts and how that relationship changes depending on whether the context is an English or biology class. Notice that this framework does not make first-year composition instructors responsible for recreating those communities of social practice (i.e., various disciplines) since to do so, in David Russell's words, would be "over ambitious" (Russell 1995, 51). Instead, first-year composition becomes about preparing students to productively engage with texts in a range of disciplines. Although Russell rightly maintains that students must actually participate in any given discipline in order to truly learn and understand that particular context and its associated conventions, this does not mean that first-year writing instructors cannot foster an *awareness* of those contexts and conventions and give students opportunities to experiment with and reflect on which reading practices work most productively in various contexts. As noted above, transfer of learning scholarship indicates that this awareness needs to be fostered, and is most successfully fostered, within a metacognitive framework. This is where Beach's discussion of generalizing is particularly useful because he underscores the "changing relations between individuals and social activities" (Beach 1999, 113) rather than seeing "transfer" as a direct, one-way application of learning or knowledge from one context to another. Drawing on this more dynamic understanding of transfer, mindful reading compels students to imagine a reciprocal relationship between themselves and any given context within which they read and compels them to reflect on that relationship. Within this mindful reading framework—as detailed in the following chapter—students are given opportunities to reflect not only on the changing contexts they encounter as they make their way through the curriculum, but how these contexts constantly change and (re)position them as readers.

The point I seek to make here regarding the dynamic process of simultaneously changing contexts and readers' positions is not unlike Anis Bawarshi's (2003) rationale for focusing on genre analysis in first-year composition. In his co-authored book, Bawarshi and Mary Jo Reiff explain that when genre is defined as more than its formal elements, as a container of sorts, "an approach to teaching writing via genre analysis, then, functions to simultaneously bring multiple knowledge domains—subject matter, rhetorical knowledge, discourse community knowledge, and writing process knowledge—into dynamic interaction. (Barawshi and Reiff 2004, 191). It is useful to think about the contexts to which I refer as these knowledge domains and substitute "reading knowledge" for "writing knowledge." In fact, both Bawarshi's pedagogy focused on genre analysis and my own focus on the mindful reading framework, which I develop more concretely in the following chapter, are committed to the potential metacognitive benefits associated with each pedagogy because they often promote transfer across contexts.[4]

While context should not be ignored, and is not ignored within a mindful reading framework, it is my contention, following scholars such as Julie Foertsch, that the dichotomy between local (i.e., context-bound) and general knowledge is often misleading if not overstated. Foertsch maintains not only that generalizable knowledge exists, but that it is, in fact, recognizable and useful, particularly as novices within disciplines develop into experts. Foertsch points out that "both generic cognitive strategies [that emphasize similarities across contexts] . . . and socially situated strategies like those seen in writing-across-the-curriculum courses have had some share of success in the classroom—and some failures, too," which leads her to use research from cognitive psychology to argue that neither approach, alone, would be most effective: "A teaching approach that uses higher level abstractions and specific examples *in combination* will be more effective in promoting transfer of learning"

(Foertsch 1995, 364, emphasis in original). Foertsch explains further, "According to the latest evidence, general knowledge and specialized knowledge arise from the same pool of memories, the same set of learning experiences" (364), which potentially means that "the general principles of academic writing should be taught in conjunction with, not separate from, contextualized examples of how those principles may be applied" (377). This approach that depends upon intertwining the construction of both generic and specific knowledge may also be the most effective way of teaching reading. In fact, Perkins and Salomon (1989, 21) note that "reading *is* a general cognitive skill which people routinely transfer to new subject matters, beginning to read in a domain with their general vocabulary and reading tactics and, as they go along, acquiring new domain-specific words, concepts, and reading tactics." Because reading is a general cognitive skill that also depends on domain-specific knowledge, Perkins and Salomon, like Foertsch, call for the "intimate intermingling of generality and context-specificity in instruction" (24). Thus, as described in more detail below and in the following chapter, within the framework of mindful reading, students would have the opportunity to conduct a close reading, for example, as it is defined by English studies, but also to imagine the general principles of close reading that are transferable across seemingly different contexts.

The importance of this combination of general and context-bound knowledge is supported by education scholars Shanahan, Shanahan, and Misischia's (2011) study. The study traced how (expert) readers—across disciplinary lines—approach disciplinary-specific texts and found that these readers do rely on disciplinary specific reading approaches, but that there are reading approaches they have in common, as well, that transcend their disciplines. After using think aloud protocols to analyze the reading habits of professors in chemistry, history, and mathematics, Shanahan and her colleagues found "many instances in which they engaged in similar strategies (sourcing, contextualization, corroboration, critiquing of the argument, use of text structure, paying attention to visual or graphical information and chemical and mathematical equations), but to varying degrees and in unique ways. They used these strategies differently and sometimes even for different purposes" (Shanahan, Shanahan and Misischia 2011, 424). While they unfortunately emphasize the not-particularly-surprising differences that exist because of disciplinary-specific conventions rather than the similarities (that might help us to generalize from one discipline to another), this exploratory research suggests that although reading strategies may be used to "varying degrees and in unique ways" across disciplines, there is, in fact, overlap among the approaches used by expert readers in disciplines as varied as history and mathematics. Particularly interesting for those of us in composition who may teach "close reading," is that "all of these experts demonstrated a 'close' reading of the texts (i.e., they analyzed particular words, sentences, and paragraphs rather than merely reading for the gist), [but] it was only the mathematicians who overtly mentioned that this was a particular strategy that they used in reading" (421). Shanahan et al. (2011) explain further: "By close reading, the mathematicians meant a reading that thoughtfully weighed the implications of nearly every word. One of the mathematicians, for example, said it usually took at least 4 or 5 hours to work his way through a single journal article for the first time. The other said that it sometimes took him years to work through a theorem so that he clearly understood it—a reason why the field does not place a high value on contemporaneousness" (421). This description of the presence of close reading in the field of mathematics reminded me that I know woefully little about what and how mathematicians read. Still, the idea that mathematicians not only read in this way, but articulate "close reading" as a particular approach is exciting because it suggests that there may exist the potential opportunity for transfer of reading knowledge from courses as radically different as first-year composition and mathematics. For while Shanahan and her colleagues are not prepared to conclude "whether these strategies can be taught to students in any way that will effectively improve their academic performance" (424), the shared terminology itself necessarily creates a connection between the two fields and an opportunity to teach for transfer across fields as seemingly disparate as composition and mathematics.

Within the context of transfer of learning studies, though, these fields are not all that different, particularly at their elementary levels where practice in the fundamentals of reading and mathematics transfer readily from one context to the next. As Carl Bereiter explains in "A Dispositional View of Transfer," "It is worth noting that there are vast areas in which transfer is not a problem at all and where it is so straightforward that no one bothers to do research on it. Reading is a highly transferable skill. . . . The same is true of writing and also of arithmetic" (Bereiter 1995, 26). He goes on to offer an important qualification: "Where transfer is problematic is in the higher level skills of reading comprehension, written composition, and mathematical problem solving. Much remains to be found out about how to achieve effective transfer at these levels" (26–27). Of course, this chapter is concerned with those higher level skills (although not those limited to comprehension) associated with reading, as is the majority of the scholarship on the transfer of writing knowledge. Although Bereiter offers the above qualification and calls for more research, the problem may be more significant than he lets on, precisely *because* reading is often seen by instructors (and students) as an elementary skill. For these instructors, transfer does not resonate as "a problem at all" even as they recognize their students' difficulties working with the course readings in their writing assignments. For students, this notion that if one can read at all one can read everything in all contexts encourages students to rely, uncritically, on default reading practices they have cultivated over the years that are not equally useful across all contexts. In the final chapter of this book, I lay out, in detail, the mindful reading framework I allude to throughout this chapter. This framework is situated as a means to both helping first-year composition instructors deliberately teach for transfer, as well as a means to combating students' uncritical (but understandable) reliance on potentially ineffective reading practices.

NOTES

1. It is worth noting that historically, within the field of education, there have been debates about whether learning transfers at all from one context to the next. The earliest (primarily physical) experiments conducted by educational psychologists Edward Thorndike and Robert Woodworth in 1901 found transfer to be rare and only successful when there were "identical elements" in the situations or contexts. Thorndike and Woodworth's theory and similar theories, which dominated the field for the first two-thirds of the twentieth century, "limit[ed] the extent to which transfer might be expected. Further, given the focus on general—context-, species-, and age-independent—laws of learning it was uninformative about mechanisms that would explain individual differences in transfer" (Campione, Shapiro, and Brown 1995, 36). In 1908, however, educational psychologist Charles Judd sought to challenge Thorndike and Woodworth's findings by asking young children to throw darts at an underwater target at different depths. The experimental group of children received instruction about how water refracted light and the control group practiced but received no instruction. The students in the experimental group were successful in doing so. Thus, his experiment yielded at least two important conclusions that separated his work from Thorndike and Woodworth's, namely that transfer was possible in situations that were not characterized by identical elements and the learner herself was an important component as one considered the possibility and probability of transfer (Haskell 2001, 81). The emphasis on the individual learner as an active participant in the process of transfer, as well as on the general principles (rather than the specifics) associated with a task might be understood as a "precursor to the metacognition approach" (Haskell 2001, 81) upon which chapter 6 draws in order to develop its "mindful reading" approach. While the vast majority of educators maintain that the whole system of education depends upon the concept of transfer (e.g., students transfer what they learn in lower-level curricular courses to higher-level ones), a rare voice that questions transfer within and beyond educational settings is Douglas K. Detterman. In the introduction to a collection of essays entitled *Transfer on Trial*, he argues that "significant transfer is probably rare and accounts for very little human behavior" (Detterman 1993, 21).

2. For an overview of relevant scholarship on transfer see Kara Taczak's (2012) "The Question of Transfer."

3. There are studies in the field of education on how reading comprehension skills transfer, particularly in early school settings. For example, see Palinscar and Brown's (1984) "Reciprocal Teaching of Comprehension-Fostering and Comprehension-Monitoring Activities" and Duke and Pearson's (2011) "Essential Elements of Fostering and Teaching Reading Comprehension."

4. For more on the relationship between genre analysis and metacognition see Devitt, Reiff, and Bawarshi's (2004) textbook *Scenes of Writing*, Bawarshi's *Genre and the Invention of the Writer*, and Bazerman's (2009) "Genre and Cognitive Development: Beyond Writing to Learn."

6

TEACHING MINDFUL READING TO PROMOTE THE TRANSFER OF READING KNOWLEDGE

Keeping the scholarship on transfer detailed in the previous chapter in mind, as well as first-year instructors' investment in teaching for transfer, this chapter contends that composition instructors should be promoting the development of metacognitive practices that help students develop knowledge *about* reading, knowledge that will prove useful as they move among contexts and classes. As it explores this particular way of making students more conscious readers, this chapter does not promote a particular reading approach such as critical reading or close reading. Neither does it seek to add mindful reading to the list of reading approaches that have been listed throughout this book. In other words, mindfully reading involves enacting a theory of reading; it is not simply another name for reading or another type of reading. As mentioned in the previous chapter, mindful reading is best understood as a framework within which instructors teach *their* chosen reading approaches. Influenced by the scholars in the 1980s and 1990s who shifted the field's attention toward *how* readers make meaning, I use the term "mindful" to underscore the metacognitive basis of this frame wherein students become *knowledgeable, deliberate,* and *reflective* about *how* they read and the demands that contexts place on their reading.

Mindful reading is related to "mindfulness," a concept often associated with Buddhism and used frequently in the field of psychology. In "The Integration of Mindfulness and Psychology," Shauna Shapiro describes mindfulness as "an abiding presence or awareness, a deep *knowing* . . . [and] the systematic

DOI: 10.7330/9780874219609.c006

practice of intentionally attending in an open, caring, and discerning way" (Shapiro 2009, 556, emphasis in original). Ellen Langer, who has researched and published numerous books and articles on mindfulness and, specifically on mindful learning for decades now, describes being mindful as the "simple act of drawing novel distinctions. It leads us," she writes, "to greater sensitivity to context and perspective. When we engage in mindful learning, we avoid forming mind-sets that unnecessarily limit us" (Langer 2000, 220). The term "mindful," when modifying reading, describes a particular stance on the part of the reader, one that is characterized by intentional awareness of and attention to the present moment, its context and one's perspective.[1] The reader's stance is crucial to my introduction of the term "mindful" into discussions about reading. While the various definitions of "metacognitive" and "mindful" often overlap, and "metacognitive" is already widely used, the concept of mindfulness highlights not just the task that one does "mindfully," but the individual, the reader, who is learning *to be* mindful. Mindfulness, unlike metacognition, is a way of being. One learns to be mindful, to adopt certain behaviors like those described by Langer. Thus, if we are interested in teaching to facilitate transfer, the term "mindful" opens up opportunities for talking about ways to cultivate mindful readers in first-year composition courses, *students* that will potentially remain mindful readers throughout their academic careers and beyond by creating the knowledge about themselves as readers. Adapting Stephen North's (not uncontroversial) statement, we might think about this in terms of producing mindful readers, not just mindful (or metacognitive) readings. It is also worth noting, that while my use of the term "mindful" draws on the definitions above, it has less in common with how compositionists interested in the relationships between spirituality and (the teaching of) writing, have been using the term. For example, Kurt Spellmeyer, Elizabeth Flynn, and Gesa E. Kirsch, who spoke on a panel at the 2013 CCCCs entitled "Occupy Writing: Meditation and the Politics of Mindfulness in the Classroom," described their investment in mindfulness as related to meditation and spirituality while my use of the term emphasizes its metacognitive associations as opposed to its spiritual connotations.[2]

My emphasis in this chapter on teaching students *how to learn* to read rather than arguing for a particular reading approach, such as rhetorical or close reading, is modeled on Elizabeth Wardle and Doug Downs' theory that rather than teaching students "how to write," which suggests that there is such a thing as good writing across all contexts, we should teach them "'*how to learn*' to write" (Wardle and Downs 2010, 21). Their "writing about writing" (WAW) approach, which teaches students "about writing" rather than teaching them writing per se is useful in hypothesizing the difference that a mindful reading framework might make to students since Wardle and Downs' WAW pedagogy also draws heavily on transfer of learning studies. In fact, one of the foundational arguments for their WAW pedagogy is that it fosters the transfer of learning by *generalizing principles* of writing rather than expecting students to develop mastery in one. While Wardle and Downs are primarily concerned with writing, Downs has alluded to the importance of a related reading pedagogy, but has yet to fully develop or describe one.[3]

Rather than thinking about which *type* of reading to teach in first-year composition, which often becomes the focus of scholarship about reading in first-year composition, we would be wise to reframe the question altogether, following the lead of Wardle and Downs. They are not interested in which *type* of writing to teach students in their first year, but rather how they can help students *construct knowledge about* writing in order to prepare students to effectively use this knowledge to make determinations about their writing in various and future contexts. Similarly, mindful reading offers the framework for supporting students' construction of knowledge *about* reading. Using transfer research from psychology, it would seem that because mindful reading supports students' generation of knowledge about reading, this approach may be a more effective way of preparing students to read in a range of contexts as opposed to teaching them a single or even several reading approaches *without* a metacognitive framework. Wardle describes the role that metacognition plays in the WAW pedagogy, useful also as a way for thinking about the potential importance of metacognition to the teaching of reading for transfer:

> Transfer research from other fields, as well as findings of my study, suggest that *meta-awareness about writing, language, and rhetorical strategies* in FYC may be the most important ability our courses can cultivate. We cannot prepare students for every genre, nor can we know every assignment they will be given or the genre conventions appropriate to those assignments across the disciplines. That knowledge—and the supports for learning it—must be gained in discipline-specific classrooms. What FYC can do, however, is help students think about writing in the university, the varied conventions of different disciplines, and their own writing strategies in light of various assignments and conventions. (Wardle 2007, 82, emphasis in original)

As might be expected in light of this approach's emphasis on facilitating students' development of knowledge *about* writing, Wardle and Downs' widely-circulating textbook *Writing about Writing* does not teach students "how to write [or] contain step-by-step advice about how to draft . . . or how to conduct research." Instead, it aims to teach students "what's going on with [their] writing and how writing works" (Wardle and Downs 2011, 1). The reading pedagogy I call for has certainly not been tested in the ways WAW curricula have (although I use it in my own courses in ways I detail at the end of this chapter). Still, the WAW movement is useful in hypothesizing the potential value therein and benefits of teaching *about* reading rather than focusing on developing students' expertise in a single reading approach, whatever that approach may be.

MINDFUL READING: A CLOSER LOOK AT THIS FRAMEWORK FOR TEACHING READING IN FIRST-YEAR COMPOSITION

In the framework of mindful reading I am calling for, rhetorical reading—and all reading approaches (e.g., close reading, critical reading)—become the composition course's subjects of inquiry. In other words, instructors would focus with students not only on which types of reading they have chosen to teach,[4] but *why* and *how* each type of reading works in specific ways. Those who continue to write about reading-writing connections often remain focused on *different types of reading* rather than the possibility of teaching students *about* reading. Bunn (2011) advocates "reading like a writer"; Ira James Allen (2012) describes the importance of teaching reading as "negotiating uncertainty"; Kathleen McCormick encourages the recognition of cognitive, expressivist, and social-cultural models of reading, ultimately supporting the latter; and Nancy Morrow (1997) provides perhaps the most comprehensive topography of reading that she thinks should be cultivated in students, including "reading to build an intellectual repertoire; reading for the unexpected; reading for the play of language; reading for strategies of persuasion; and reading for genre conventions." Morrow notes, however, that "no one course could possibly explore all of these ways of reading" (n.p.).

Contrary to Morrow's position, I contend not only that composition instructors could explore multiple ways of reading in a single course, but that they *must* if they want their students to have the tools to read both widely and deeply in and beyond first-year composition. This means that instructors would be responsible for exposing students to texts, as well as accompanying reading and writing assignments that make different demands on them. Asking students to consider what rhetorically reading (however an instructor defines that) a text enables them to notice and comment on in comparison to what close reading (again, however an instructor defines that) gives students access to multiple approaches. More importantly, it gives them the opportunity to develop knowledge about each approach individually, their relationship to that approach, as well as knowledge about that approach in comparison to others. This helps students develop the metacognitive skills useful for moving among reading approaches in deliberate and mindful ways.

I want to pause for a bit in order to further develop this notion of mindful reading through a familiar example. Let's say a student in a first-year composition course is assigned Paulo Freire's "The 'Banking' Concept of Education," a chapter from *Pedagogy of the Oppressed*, as they sometimes are, particularly if *Ways of Reading* is the course's textbook. Based on how the instructors I spoke with teach rhetorical reading, this student would be responsible for determining Freire's purpose and audience, among other rhetorical aspects of the text. On the one hand, these seem like elements that students who are reading rhetorically might readily be able to point to and even support with evidence from the text. For example, reading rhetorically may help students recognize that one of Freire's purposes is to expose and critique the common conception of the relationship between teachers and students wherein the former have all of the knowledge and the latter are simply the passive containers in which teachers will make deposits. Reading rhetorically may even allow students to make connections between the two parts of Freire's chapter, namely the first part about the teacher-student relationship and the second, more difficult part that provides the very abstract Marxist-driven foundation for his conception of critical pedagogy, as well as his critique of education as a *system*. But, at a certain point, rhetorical reading breaks down as an approach and no longer provides adequate access to the text's complexities, particularly those that arise in this second part of the chapter wherein Freire develops concepts such as "conscientização," "praxis," "consciousness as consciousness of consciousness," "*intentionality* of consciousness," "dialogical relations," "cognitive actors," and "humanization." I use these terms as indications of one of the text's complexities (rather than simply terms that need to be defined) that cannot be accessed and, therefore, deliberately worked with via rhetorical reading alone. In other words, it does not seem to me that reading rhetorically would help students understand these difficult, abstract concepts. This exposes a few problems. First, if students are only taught one way of reading—let's say rhetorical reading—then they don't have the tools to make sense of these ideas that are crucial to understanding Freire's chapter. Second, even if students are taught multiple ways of reading, but without a

metacognitive framework like mindful reading, they are potentially unaware of when a certain reading approach is failing
them and it is time to introduce a different approach. Thus, I
am not arguing that the answer is to teach students as many ways
of reading as we can fit into a semester (although I do think that
the more approaches we can give them the better we prepare
them to work with unfamiliar discourses). Instead, we need to
help students recognize at what moment in their reading process they need to relinquish a particular reading approach and
introduce an alternative one and why. Educational psychologist
Michael Pressley describes in a more general sense what this process looks like, particularly for younger students, who have been
the subject of most reading research: "Good strategy users evaluate whether the strategies they are using are producing progress
toward goals they have set for themselves." Moreover, they are
able to recognize the "benefits that follow from using the procedures and the amount of effort required to carry out strategies"
(Pressley 1990, 9). Applied to reading, students would be able
to identify specific moments in complex texts when they need to
shift reading approaches, and they need to have enough knowledge and practice with various approaches in order to make
informed decisions about the approach they will abandon and
that which they will introduce in its place. In order to more comprehensively explore how the concept of mindfulness can help
students reach this goal, I include the following passage, in its
entirety, from Langer's (2000, 220) "Mindful Learning":

> Mindfulness is a flexible state of mind in which we are actively
> engaged in the present, noticing new things and sensitive to
> context. When we are in a state of mindlessness, we act like
> automatons who have been programmed to act according to the
> sense our behavior made in the past, rather than the present.
> Instead of actively drawing new distinctions, noticing new things,
> as we do when we are mindful, when we are mindless we rely
> on distinctions drawn in the past. We are stuck in a single, rigid
> perspective, and we are oblivious to alternative ways of knowing.
> When we are mindless, our behavior is rule and routine gov-
> erned; when we are mindful, rules and routines may guide our
> behavior rather than predetermine it.

Teaching reading within the metacognitive framework I am calling for means sensitizing students to that particular context and encouraging them to reflect on the present moment, how far a reading approach takes them, what aspects of the text it allows them to address, and what meanings it enables and prohibits. Rather than reading "mindlessly" or perhaps relying on their default or a rigid way of reading other texts, students benefit from the flexibility that mindful reading offers in that it compels them to actively draw on a repertoire of reading approaches they have been cultivating in first-year composition.

Students might represent and reflect on their reading processes and their movement among reading approaches in reading journals and other related assignments. I have students explore why a reading approach only takes them so far, what that tells them about the approach, as well as about themselves as readers. Moreover, I also ask students to dwell on the moments when a particular approach fails them and consider why it has, what this tells them about the reading approach, the text, and themselves. These metacognitive considerations shift attention toward more generalizable issues surrounding how and why particular reading approaches function as they do. While I do not mean to downplay the selection and teaching of particular reading approaches such as rhetorical reading, close reading, or any of the types of reading Morrow and others list, as educational and cognitive psychologists find, metacognition is key to "positive transfer" wherein "learning in one context enhances and improves a related performance in another context" (Perkins and Salomon 1992). Reading knowledge is less likely to transfer from one context to the next unless students are constructing this knowledge within a metacognitive framework that fosters generalization.

The knowledge about reading that students are constructing has the potential to transfer across disciplinary boundaries as they work within a range of unfamiliar discourses. When reading an article in the sciences, for example, a student may readily understand the piece's description of an experiment, but as the article gets more abstract in its analysis that initial reading approach may no longer work. If the student recognizes what is happening in that moment of difficulty, namely that the initial reading approach is beginning to "fail," then the student can work through that difficulty by drawing on his knowledge about other reading approaches that would be more effective at that moment. The student, in Langer's (2000, 220) words, would not get "stuck in a single, rigid perspective" and would, instead, become open to "alternative ways of knowing."

Often scholarship on transfer encourages instructors to anticipate *for* students which aspects of assignments and activities will transfer most readily to other courses, but I have found that giving students opportunities to do this work can be even more powerful. Because students are more familiar with their other classes and their major (if they have declared one) than I am, they are actually much better at anticipating the ways in which they might transfer this knowledge. Moreover, they are often also successful at looking back at assignments from other classes, including those in high school, in order to imagine how what they know now about reading may have helped them then. A few short writing assignments throughout the course of the semester that ask students to reflect in this manner can go a long way toward helping them make connections (that can facilitate transfer) between first-year composition and other current, past, and future academic courses.

This mindful reading framework also has the potential to motivate students to complete the course readings, which is crucial in order for students to even have opportunities to transfer their reading knowledge. Bunn's, Jolliffe and Harl's, and my study all corroborate that students need to see that the reading they do is directly connected to their writing in order to feel motivated to complete the course's reading assignments. Within the framework I am calling for, students' reading—or more precisely reading knowledge—is overtly and deliberately connected not only to current writing assignments, but to future reading and writing activities. As Anne Beaufort and Elizabeth Wardle both found in their research, even when students described their first-year writing courses as valuable, they were largely unable to generalize and thus imagine how that writing connected to other courses: "They did not appear to make even near connections of those skills, much less transfer those skills to very different contexts. For example, no students suggested they were being asked to write a persuasive paper in order to be able to write persuasively in other courses" (Wardle 2009, 777). While Wardle is lamenting the lack of transfer of writing knowledge, the same may follow for reading knowledge unless first-year writing instructors teach reading within the sort of mindful reading framework for which I am calling.

I would argue—with a plea for research in this area—that based on transfer of learning scholarship and the research that supports WAW pedagogy we might hypothesize the following: Unless we teach reading with an eye toward helping students develop an awareness of which approaches or combination thereof might be the most productive within future and different contexts then we are only preparing them to succeed in our courses. While we may disagree about the goals of first-year composition, I don't think any of us would argue for teaching that is only applicable and valuable for the months that these students are with us in our classrooms. And, increasingly, we are expected to articulate—if not defend—through "objective" evidence the value of our teaching methods.

While compositionists may gravitate first to anecdotal evidence when talking about the need to support the improvement of our students' reading abilities, my call for a reexamination and a re-envisioning of how reading is being taught in first-year composition is supported by recent findings from The Citation Project, a multi-institutional, empirical research project that seeks to understand how students read sources and use them in their writing. Rebecca Moore Howard, Tricia Serviss, and Tanya K. Rodrigue (2010) describe their pilot study in their article "Writing from Sources, Writing from Sentences." In this initial study, no student in the sample pool actually uses summary. Instead, they write from sentences not from sources, relying on paraphrasing, copying, citing, and what Moore calls patchwriting. In Sandra Jamieson and Rebecca Moore Howard's follow-up study of students' writing from 16 U. S. colleges and universities, only six-percent of students' citations were to summary, summary that usually focused on a very limited amount of text. These findings, thus, raise questions about "whether students understand the sources they are citing in their researched writing" (Howard, Serviss, and Rodrigue 2010, 189). Howard, Serviss, and Rodrigue also note, "The absence of summary, coupled with the exclusive engagement of text on the sentence level, means that readers have no assurance that the students *did* read and understand" (186). Although their findings are intended to help educators reconceive how they think about plagiarism, the data suggest that post-secondary students have extreme difficulty reading and understanding the texts they encounter. Moreover, the pilot study suggested, and the later study confirmed, that "it was consistently the sentences not the sources students were writing from" (189) as students were constructing arguments "from isolated sentences pulled from sources" (188). This lack of attention to context has significant consequences not just for academic integrity and instruction in research-based writing, but also for instruction in reading. Students, it would seem, are reading without attending to context in any significant way. Students "sear[ch] for 'good sentences'" (189) to integrate into their writing, but ignore the context in which these sentences appear. Teaching various reading approaches within the mindful reading framework I am calling for sensitizes students to context by compelling them to become aware of the relationship between context and their reading practices.

THE IMPORTANCE OF TEACHING READING WITHIN A METACOGNITIVE FRAMEWORK

Some scholars (e.g., Bunn, Allen, McCormick, and Morrow) who write about the role of reading in writing instruction advocate the teaching of specific reading approaches. While their methods for arriving at their conclusions differ, these scholars ultimately declare a single approach or a handful of approaches they deem to be the most productive for inclusion in composition courses. This is important work, and I find their rationales for incorporating their specific reading approaches into composition courses convincing. This scholarship, though, is almost exclusively focused only on the composition classroom without thought toward the role that teaching reading in this general education course might play as students make their way beyond first-year composition. Certainly, instructors need to teach students the approaches that will serve them well in their particular courses and immediate contexts. Teaching rhetorical reading through the use of models may, in fact, be one of the most concrete and productive ways of connecting students' reading to the writing, which is crucial to motivate students to read for their writing courses and to experience the relationship between these two practices. But, this book contends that it is time to move away from simply *naming* one approach superior to others since research on the transfer of learning suggests that it is the *framework* within which teaching and learning occur that largely determines if and how that learning translates into other and future contexts. This perspective cannot continued to be ignored when considering a general education course such as first-year composition.

Thus, when we think about first-year composition as a general education course, some of the questions we ask about reading instruction necessarily change. It is no longer adequate to consider only how specific reading approaches will benefit students within the immediate context of that course. While connecting students' reading to their writing in overt and deliberate ways is a first step and crucial way of motivating students to complete that reading, and perhaps even improve their writing, it is only a first step. As experts in teaching and learning scholarship in general education programs, Ruth Benander, English professor, and Robin Lightner, psychology professor note, making "transfer expectations explicit" (Benander and Lightner 2005, 203) is also important. They continue, "Reminding [students] that transfer is expected can go a long way to promoting transfer. Explicitly talking about these expectations in class, especially for first-year students, can help students know that they need to think more broadly" (204). Thus, within the context of general education and transfer of learning studies, the question of which type of reading compositionists should privilege is not necessarily the most productive one to ask. My refusal to take a position on which type of reading to teach follows from this perspective that suggests that instructors should help their students cultivate a repertoire of reading approaches and a means for making decisions about which contexts demand which approaches. To teach in this way is actually more challenging than teaching a single reading approach since it involves helping students develop ways of reading that are characterized by rhetorical adaptability. Although more challenging for the instructor, its potential benefits seem better aligned with the goals of the first-year writing instructors who worry about the extent to which they are preparing their students for future courses and contexts. To make a case for a single approach would be to deny the scholarship that comes from fields like educational and cognitive psychology, interdisciplinary research on the transfer of learning, as well as the research conducted on general education courses and programs. Declaring the teaching of a single reading approach as better than all of the others is far too limiting and, just as important, teaching any reading approach without a metacognitive framework is not likely to prepare students for reading outside of that single composition course. A framework along the lines of the mindful reading one I describe gives instructors the freedom to teach students the reading approaches that will be useful in that specific context while simultaneously developing students' abilities to generalize those approaches, which will benefit them throughout their academic careers and beyond.

As we work toward teaching our students to be mindful of the contexts within which they read, and the flexibility and adaptability those contexts demand, we would be wise to begin looking beyond the context of composition to some of these related fields in order to better understand—as did scholars in the 1980s and 1990s—what compositionists might draw on from their research to develop its own research questions and studies on reading.

Looking ahead, it is important as a field to continue considering in more depth the most commonly reported reading approaches currently taught in first-year composition. We might start by exploring those approaches that emerged from my national study detailed in chapter 2. As we do so, though, we need to ask questions about these approaches, questions that are informed by a commitment to teaching reading approaches that are transferrable to other contexts and to teaching in ways that help students recognize transferability.

If part of this revival of interest in reading involves imagining how instructors can facilitate their students' transfer of reading knowledge, something on the minds of the majority of instructors I interviewed, then the field of composition needs to conduct some of its own research that can provide insight into the relationship between the transfer of writing knowledge and the transfer of reading knowledge. We can learn a great deal from the scholars from the 1980s and 1990s who studied and developed reading pedagogies, many of which depend upon metacognitive activities. While these scholars were not overtly interested in issues of transfer, their pedagogies remain recoverable and useful as we consider the issues outlined in this chapter. Berthoff and Salvatori's double- and triple-entry notebook assignments, which encourage students to self-monitor as they read, as well as Salvatori's "difficulty paper," which compels students to confront and reflect on the difficulties they encounter, are some of the assignments that emerged during this time that support the metacognitive framework I am describing. Below, by way of concluding this chapter, I outline two assignments and offer a handful of readings that can be used to support this mindful reading pedagogy in composition classes.

ASSIGNMENTS THAT SUPPORT MINDFUL READING

As I imagined this book, I found myself hesitant to include assignments that demonstrate how I put into practice the mindful reading pedagogy I outline just above. I certainly did not want to fall into the trap that Berthoff describes as "recipe-swapping" wherein instructors diminish the theoretical aspect of teaching by simply sharing decontextualized assignments and practices with each other. As Berthoff (1981b, 68) aptly describes, "learning to write is a matter of theoretical consideration, not just recipe swapping" and to uncritically privilege the practical component diminishes not only what happens in the classroom, but the field of composition as a whole. Mariolina Salvatori has also described the consequences of privileging only the practical aspect of teaching: "The reduction of pedagogy from a philosophical science to a repertoire of 'tips for teaching,' shows that our educational system has consistently opted for simplifying solutions every time it has been confronted with the inherent and inescapable complexity of educational issues" (Salvatori 1996b, 452). Still, one of the most prevalent comments made by first-year writing instructors during my interviews with them was that they longed for help, for support, as they imagined how to better integrate attention to reading into their writing courses. They wanted new ways of incorporating reading into their classes and ideas for assessing and potentially revising what they are already doing. Because this book is intended to help reanimate composition's interest in reading pedagogies and offer support for those first-year instructors who are already integrating attention to reading in their classes, I feel compelled to briefly share some of the ways I have put into practice the mindful reading pedagogy I describe. I include this brief discussion of a few assignments to lend specificity to my above discussion rather than to be prescriptive. And, I do so with an important caveat inspired by Berthoff and Salvatori's concerns: These assignments are part of a larger framework wherein reading plays as much a role as writing in a first-year composition course. To yank these assignments from this context and incorporate them into a first-year writing course that is not committed to a pedagogy based on mindful reading or similar theoretical notion is not likely to "work." In other words, the success of these assignments and activities depends upon their integration into first-year composition courses that attend to reading deliberately and consistently.

Robert Scholes has pointed out that perhaps the biggest challenge involved in teaching reading is that the process of reading remains largely invisible, unlike writing: "We normally acknowledge, however grudgingly, that writing must be taught and continue to be taught from high school to college and perhaps beyond. We accept it, I believe, because we can see writing, and we know that much of the writing we see is not good enough. But we do not see reading. We see some writing about reading, to be sure, but we do not see reading. I am certain, though, that if we could see it, we would be appalled" (Scholes 2002, 166). If we are going to foreground the relationship between reading and writing in our first-year writing courses (and ultimately beyond those courses), we must find ways of making reading as visible as writing so we can work as deliberately on reading as we do on writing. The following assignments help foreground reading and do so within a framework intended to foster metacognition and the positive transfer of reading knowledge.

1. The Passage-Based Paper (PBP): Teaching Close Reading within a Mindful Reading Framework

For more than a decade, one of the assignments I have used most consistently to make reading visible is the passage-based paper (PBP for short).[5] I have revised the assignment in different ways over the years and, most recently, to reflect the mindful reading framework within which I have been teaching. The following assignment, which students are asked to complete throughout the term, is distributed to them at the start of the semester:

What Is A Passage-Based Paper (PBP)?
Throughout the course of the semester, I will ask that you choose a short passage (*three to five* sentences) from the text that we are reading and write a *one to two* page passage-based paper on this excerpt. You will be expected to discuss this passage in class, reflect on your PBP, and hand in the assignment at the end of class.

Format: Transcribe the passage onto the top of the page (including the page number from which the passage is taken) and then "unpack" the passage, paying close attention to the textual elements including the passage's language, tone, and construction. Once you have examined the passage closely, conclude your paper by connecting this passage to the rest of the work. In other words, once you have completed a close, textual analysis of your passage, contemplate the meaning of the passage and its place in or contribution to the meaning(s) of the text as a whole.

Purpose: Passage-based papers offer you the opportunity to experience the connections between the interpretive practices of reading and writing. These papers give you the opportunity to engage in close textual analysis and to grapple with difficult ideas that come up in the texts that we will be reading. I am concerned primarily with your ability to work closely with the texts that we are reading, practice that will be useful to you beyond this course. We are working with difficult texts and it is fine if your papers represent an attempt at developing an argument through close analysis of a passage as opposed to a fully-developed argument. These passage-based papers also prepare you for writing formal essays in this class and beyond, in which you will be expected to attend to textual evidence as carefully as you attend to the passages you choose for your passage-based papers.

Preparation and Support: At the beginning of the term, we will work together on writing passage-based papers. We will discuss strategies for choosing a passage and completing these assignments. You will receive feedback on your PBPs from me, as well as from your peers.

A challenge for most students in part because they are far more accustomed to traditional response papers that do not insist that they focus solely on the text and the textual elements therein, the PBP gives students the opportunity to offer a sustained reading of a short excerpt, to single out a passage they believe to be rich with meaning and then offer a reading that is based on the elements present in that passage. The passage-based paper allows me to see and comment upon students' reading practices. And, because we are working with a very small portion of text, my comments are necessarily specific in nature as I respond to a student's very local reading. Keeping reading this contained, I am able to see how students proceed in their readings: how they move from looking at certain words and phrases to making claims about them. This assignment makes students slow down and become aware of the process by which they make meaning, and it allows me to see and comment on this meaning making.

Within the framework of mindful reading, the PBP can be used to help students generalize the elements of the assignment so that they can imagine an application of these in different contexts. A close reading assignment, the PBP gives students the experience of paying close attention to textual elements in order to construct meaning. Notice that there is nothing necessarily "literary" about what students comment upon in the text. Instead, the PBP encourages students to cultivate an awareness of the relationship among language, style, and meaning. This sort of work is relevant in all disciplines because students are often learning to recognize the features of and imitate writing in various disciplines. In their four year, cross-disciplinary study of student writers and instructors, Chris Thaiss and Terry Myers Zawacki found that "students can infer style by reading professional writing" (Thaiss and Zawacki 2006, 128). While inferring is certainly useful, the PBP asks students to do far more than that as students are actually writing about these textual elements in order to reveal their processes of reading.

The PBP compels students to become conscious of how close reading works and the extent to which it may be a useful approach in other courses and contexts. In order to help facilitate this transfer, I ask students to reflect on their passage-based papers in two different ways. First, they describe how they met the requirements of the assignment by listing the observations they make about the passage and the implications they draw from them. I also ask students to comment on the difficulties they faced while writing and what they are most proud of in their passage-based paper. In addition, I offer students opportunities to imagine how close attention to textual elements might be useful in their academic careers beyond first-year composition, as well as how this approach might have helped them in previous classes and contexts.[6] Because they are first-year students, many look back at their high school courses in order to imagine applications. One of my students noted that "this method would have greatly assisted in Speech class senior year of high school by ensuring that I made my arguments clear to the class and left no stone unturned on the subject of each of our assignments." Another commented, "I wish I had learned or used something like this throughout my courses [in] high school and previous college semesters. It really taught me how to analyze a passage, and focus on it, rather than having ever-broadening ideas." Finally, a third student anticipated the PBP's future uses: "I haven't had to quote anyone else's work in any papers yet in college, but . . . it will be useful when I take literature second semester." It is worth noting that not all students can imagine future (and/or past) uses of the passage-based paper, and instead, comment on how other ways of reading seem to hold more potential for them. The point is that the PBP's emphasis on close reading allows students to experience and reflect on this reading approach in comparison to others taught in first-year composition. Students can bring this experience with them to other courses and continue to develop their knowledge about what close reading enables them to notice and say about texts. The PBP, along with these accompanying metacognitive exercises, helps students *create knowledge about* close reading and begin considering its uses and assessing its value beyond first-year composition.

2. The Reading Journal: Constructing and Recording Knowledge about Reading

As described in earlier chapters, double- and triple- entry notebooks, used by Berthoff, Salvatori and Donahue ask students to identify and reflect upon different aspects of the texts they read. The reading journals that I ask students to keep support the metacognitive goals of these notebook assignments, but ultimately, they are used to help students identify, track, and reflect on the reading practices they are introduced to in first-year composition. Students are expected to complete a journal entry for each reading. Initially, before I introduce different reading practices by name, students simply describe their current reading practices in their own terms. As I introduce more formal names for our reading approaches students are expected to use these to describe their reading experiences. Students' journals become artifacts of their mindful reading as their entries reflect their answers to the following questions about each text:

- Which reading approach will I employ first and why?
- How far does this reading approach take me?
- What does this reading approach allow me to notice in the text?
- What must I ignore?
- What meanings does this approach allow me to construct and what meanings does it prohibit?

Follow-up questions that encourage students to develop knowledge about the reading strategies themselves and about their individual reading practices include:

- At what point in the reading and why did I need to abandon my initial approach?
- Why did the initial approach only take me so far?
- What does this tell me about the approach, as well as about me as a reader?
- What other approaches do I need to bring into play in order to construct a meaning that achieves the goals associated with my reading/writing assignment?
- To what extent might this reading experience be useful as I read texts in my other courses?

These questions ask students to reflect on the potential and limits of each approach within the given context. These metacognitive questions shift attention toward more generalizable considerations surrounding how and why particular reading approaches function as they do and help students learn about themselves as readers. The general questions listed above are intended to frame the more specific methods of reading, like rhetorical and close reading, that are taught in first-year composition. As students answer the general questions about the specific reading practices taught, they develop knowledge about the practices themselves and can begin to imagine how these practices might be used in multiple contexts, across disciplinary boundaries, and to different ends. Using reading journals to generalize in this way has the potential to facilitate "positive" transfer wherein "learning in one context enhances and improves a related performance in another context" (Perkins and Salomon 1992).

COURSE READINGS THAT SUPPORT THE DEVELOPMENT OF KNOWLEDGE ABOUT READING

By now it should be clear that this book's interest is in *how* we might teach reading in first-year composition rather than which texts we should teach. That latter question, though, isn't completely irrelevant, and I imagine that some of my readers may want me to address the issue of textual selection and how the readings I assign fit within this mindful reading framework meant to promote the construction of knowledge *about* reading. Many of the pieces I mention in Chapter 4 can work successfully in a first-year composition classroom focused on interrogating and practicing various reading approaches. I have found particular success with many of the pieces listed below and, in the future, I anticipate using the others that I have included on this list. Some of these titles also appear in the annotated bibliography, which includes additional information about them.

1. "The Transition to College Reading," Robert Scholes

I often use this reading at the beginning of composition courses in order to emphasize that the course will focus equally on reading and writing. It also gives me the opportunity to introduce the idea that reading and writing are connected practices. Even at the beginning of the semester students are already realizing that the reading they do in college and the expectations associated with it are different from what many of them experienced in high school. This piece about that transition allows us to address those and related issues.

2. *Rewriting: How to Do Things with Texts,* **Joseph Harris**

Each chapter in this book introduces a "move" intended to help students incorporate other voices into their writing, but the one chapter that I have found most relevant to attending to reading in a writing classroom is "Chapter 1: Coming to Terms." In this chapter, Harris describes and models the "importance of representing the work of others in ways that are both fair to them and useful to your own aims in writing" (Harris 2006, 5). Unfortunately, Harris does not address reading per se in much depth nor describe how students might read in order to achieve this. Still, because this move depends upon students' abilities to read these sources in such a way that they can accurately and productively represent them, this chapter enables class discussions about what it means to represent a source accurately and which reading practices are conducive to reaching that goal.

3. "A Relationship between Reading and Writing: The Conversation Model," Charles Bazerman

This article introduces the metaphor of academic discourse as conversation, a concept that is unfamiliar to most of my students. As does Harris in "Coming to Terms," Bazerman underscores the importance of cultivating in students "various techniques of absorbing, reformulating, commenting on, and using reading" (Bazerman 1980, 658). This article allows me to refer to academic writing as a conversation throughout the semester because students have an understanding of this concept from the article. Related to that, we become cognizant of the various ways in which one might "use" reading and the techniques and strategies that best support those uses.

4. *Writing Analytically* **(sixth edition), David Rosenwasser and Jill Stephen**

I frequently use this textbook in its entirety in my composition (both first-year and advanced) courses, but particular chapters of interest include "Chapter 2: Toolkit of Analytical Methods I: Seeing Better, Seeing More"; Chapter 3: Analysis: What it Is and What It Does"; "Chapter 4: Toolkit of Analytical Methods II: Going Deeper"; and "Chapter 5: Writing About Reading: More Moves to Make With Written Texts." These chapters offer and model for students a range of analytical "moves," or what might be called specific reading strategies, including, but not limited to the following: "suspend judgment"; "define significant parts and how they are related"; "look for patterns of repetition and contrast and for anomalies"; "make the implicit explicit"; and "keep reformulating questions and explanations" (Rosenwasser and Stephen 2011, 53). This textbook describes and models for students what they might look for and do as they read. As such, it models and concretizes for students the moves that more expert readers make almost unconsciously as they read. These strategies and techniques become part of the class's vocabulary and I ask students to consistently practice these strategies, reflect on their uses, as well as on how far each one takes them.

5. *They Say/I Say: The Moves that Matter in Academic Writing*, **Gerald Graff and Cathy Birkenstein**

This text teaches students how one goes about incorporating others' voices into their own writing. Although a writing handbook, I find this volume useful in preparing students to notice the moments in the readings where authors are incorporating other voices. This allows us to discuss how these writers are *using* their reading and even more specifically the turns of phrase that signal this. Ultimately, this leads to discussions and reflections on how this way of reading can support students as they not only read in their composition course(s), but also in other disciplines, each of which practices reading and uses readings differently.

6. "Introduction: Ways of Reading" in *Ways of Reading*, David Bartholomae, Anthony Petrosky, and Stacey Waite

Even if one does not adopt this anthology in its entirety, the introductory materials are especially useful. This rich introduction, which touches on the concept of "difficulty" and addresses specific reading practices such as reading with and against the grain, as well as the importance of second readings, can offer a useful introduction to a composition course that is focused as much on reading as on writing. It is an instructive overview of the process of reading, particularly as it applies to difficult texts, and has served as a springboard for many fruitful discussions with my students.

7. *The Elements (and Pleasures) of Difficulty*, Mariolina Rizzi Salvatori and Patricia Donahue

The first one-third of this slim textbook is particularly useful in introducing students to metacognitive exercises such as the triple-entry notebook and the importance of reflective questions. Defining reading for students as a "transaction," the early chapters of this book convey the importance of active reading, often defined by an emphasis on metacognitive reflection. I have used pieces from these chapters to help explain my own journal assignment, as well as other metacognitive activities I assign.

8. "Studying the 'Reading Transition' from High School to College: What Are Our Students Reading and Why?" David A. Joliffe and Allison Harl

Like Scholes's piece, this article addresses the transition that students experience from high school to college and is, thus, a useful piece for them to read, reflect on, and respond to early in the semester. This article also opens up discussions about what students read outside of school and allows them to begin reflecting on the relationship between those reading practices and those they apply to "school reading."

9. "From Story to Essay: Reading and Writing," Anthony Petrosky

This piece challenges the common notion that reading is only about recall. Many students bring this conception with them to the writing classroom and, thus, are ill-prepared to discuss reading and to read in the ways my courses often expect them to. Petrosky, instead, explores how reading, responding, and composing are all aspects of understanding and that what we call comprehension is actually an act of composition rather than simply information retrieval. This essay, then, has the potential to introduce alternative ways of thinking about the concept of comprehension.

10. "Reading and Writing a Text: Correlations between
Reading and Writing Patterns," Mariolina Salvatori

This article lays out for students the relationship between reading and writing and explores a case study that examines how a particular student's strides in reading were reflected in his writing. This article has the potential to enrich discussions about the relationship between the practices of reading and writing and help students understand why a course in writing would also focus on reading.

NOTES

1. For an in-depth account of its Buddhist origins, as well as more contemporary uses of the concept of mindfulness see Terry Hyland's (2011) *Mindfulness and Learning*.

2. For additional scholarship on the relationship between spirituality and literacy see Kristie S. Fleckenstein's (2003) *Embodied Literacies: Imageword and a Poetics of Teaching*, Beth Daniell's (2003) *A Community of Friendship: Literacy, Spiritual Practice and Women in Recovery*, as well as *The Journal of the Assembly for Expanded Perspectives on Learning* (*JAEPL*), which regularly publishes articles from those in composition and related fields on the relationship between the teaching of writing and meditation.

3. See Downs' (2010) "Teaching First-Year Writers to Use Texts: Scholarly Readings in Writing-about-Writing in First-Year Comp."

4. The scholarship from the 1980s and 1990s offers an overview of a range of reading approaches and outlines their benefits. For recent topographies that are useful in imagining the benefits of teaching certain reading approaches, see Nancy Morrow's and Michael Bunn's scholarship.

5.   I was introduced to a version of this assignment more than fifteen years ago by one of my undergraduate professors, Dr. James Bloom at Muhlenberg College, whose pedagogy continues to inspire my own.

6.   It is worth noting that in this example, students are both reading their own writing, as well as their own schooling experiences. In the case of reading (in order to reflect on) their own writing, they are doing so after they have composed their PBPs. There is important scholarship on the role that reading plays in the composition process, characterized, in part, by an ongoing debate as to whether reading and re-reading one's writing *as one writes* improves the writing and thinking or unnecessarily bogs one down in surface-level concerns.

7

EPILOGUE
A Changing Landscape

When I first conceived of this book in 2009 there was very little formally articulated interest in the place of reading in writing instruction other than, of course, the WPA-L discussion with which this book opens. Years had passed since articles on the subject had been published in the field's journals and books on the subject were simply not being published. As I received rejection letters from potential publishers of this manuscript, I sought advice from colleagues in the field who had success in the 1980s and 1990s publishing on reading only to find out that some of them had also recently unsuccessfully proposed manuscripts on reading to various publishers.

As I draft this epilogue in the late months of 2012, it seems as though this landscape has changed dramatically. As Mariolina Salvatori and Patricia Donahue note in their 2012 *College English* article, there seems to be a "revival" of interest in reading in composition. They describe the "handful of sessions on reading at the yearly CCCC" that "are packed once again" (Salvatori and Donahue 2012, 199). In addition, three articles on reading were published in the Winter 2012 issue of *Pedagogy*. The first and second meetings of The Role of Reading in Composition Studies Special Interest Group, which I co-founded, were well-attended in March 2012 and 2013 at the Conference on College Composition and Communication's annual meeting. We have seen the introduction of new clusters on the CCCC's proposal form that explicitly address reading in its relationship to writing, and there are forthcoming special journal issues, essay collections, and single-authored books on reading's relationship

DOI: 10.7330/9780874219609.c007

to writing. I hope that this book contributes to this revival of interest in reading within composition and that the tentative findings I outline in Chapter 2 are explored, in more depth, in the coming years. These findings might be summarized in the following way:

- Rhetorical reading is one of the most common reading approaches taught in first-year composition.
- Many first-year writing instructors use rhetorical reading to connect the processes of reading and writing often through modeling exercises.
- Many first-year writing instructors do not feel as though their graduate and professional training prepared them to attend to reading in their writing classrooms.
- First-year writing instructors want opportunities to learn more about how their students read and how they can help them become better readers.
- First-year writing instructors would like ways to assess students' reading abilities, how they affect their writing abilities, and whether they are sufficiently preparing students to read effectively in other courses.

Based on these findings, my analysis of the professional discourse about reading from the 1980s and 1990s, and on the theoretical framework offered by transfer of learning scholars, I make the following recommendations:

We must commit ourselves to studying reading in ways that are recognizable and valued outside of our discipline so that we have more opportunities to fund these studies.

As we consider how to go about studying reading within the context of composition and beyond, we would be wise to imagine what methods will be most successful in garnering funding for these studies since composition has a history of being skeptical of methods, like empiricism, that are widely accepted in other, often related disciplines. Several of the first-year writing instructors I spoke to mentioned grants or research funding they had trouble earning because of the lack of previous work in composition on reading. Carla described, in detail, her experience of developing a grant proposal. She explained that it was rejected because "there was no hard data that we could cite, no numbers we could cite that showed in measurable ways that reading enhanced writing. So we decided that if we're going to propose this again, we've got to hunt for more quantitative data. But again, it was hard to find. Yet we all know it is true [that more reading equals better writing] but we've to got to write it up, I guess." Carla and her colleagues' predicament underscores the importance of testing assumed or commonplace disciplinary "knowledge" that has gone largely untested, at least in the last two decades. As Carla and her colleagues found when they were applying for a grant, they were at a loss for evidence that would be recognized as such by a grant committee since "there were no numbers [they] could cite that showed in measurable ways that reading enhanced writing."

My own experience tells a similar story. While I was fortunate to earn a CCCC's Research Initiative Grant to support the study described in this book, I applied simultaneously for a grant from the Department of Education, which I did not receive for some of the same reasons Carla and her colleagues did not receive theirs. Writing about my proposal, the committee noted that "the literature reviewed in this application is often outdated" (2). While the CCCC's grant committee seemed to understand that I was proposing to undertake work that was absent in the field, the Department of Education—an important funding source outside of our immediate disciplinary circle—was less familiar with this dearth in the field. They suggested that there is current research and data upon which I may have drawn, but are not clear in which field I might have found this information, as it is certainly not composition. The committee, thus, assumed that the lack of "current" evidence I provided and the "outdated" scholarship I cited were oversights on my part. While compositionists are lucky to have such a supportive professional organization in the CCCCs, we need to make our work recognizable to those outside of our immediate circles or we may not be able to fund the studies that are crucial to developing new knowledge in composition and extending earlier research on reading.

In order to prepare graduate students and new instructors to study reading, we must rethink graduate education in rhetoric and composition, as well as the professional development opportunities offered to instructors.

Based on the surveys and interviews I conducted, it is clear that instructors feel ill-prepared to teach reading, but are nonetheless committed to integrating reading into their classrooms and programs. With little or no support from the field's professional discourse or from their graduate training, they have developed methods of teaching reading, but these feel shallow to them because they are not informed by recent theory or research. As such, these instructors worry about the effectiveness of their reading pedagogies.

The lack of attention to reading in current rhetoric and composition graduate courses or even separate graduate courses on the topic, something lamented by fifty-one percent of instructors I spoke to, produces scholar-teachers who, even if they are interested in focusing on reading in their composition classes, do not necessarily feel comfortable doing so because they have not been trained in that area. Moreover, even if graduate classes are using a current anthology like Miller's *Norton Book of Composition Studies* or Victor Villanueva's *Cross-Talk in Comp Theory: A Reader*, graduate students remain in the dark about the plethora of scholarship on reading from the 1980s and 1990s since neither of these texts includes essays about reading pedagogy. These students, therefore, remain largely unaware that reading research is even a topic one can pursue in composition. When they do develop an interest in the place of reading in composition, they may be faced with skepticism from others in composition. Two instructors I interviewed who sought to write dissertations on reading were confronted with much confusion by their potential dissertation directors who did not understand what reading had to do with composition and tried to persuade them otherwise. The annotated bibliography, which constitutes Appendix A, has the potential to support instructors who are interested in reading the scholarship that has been produced on this topic and to help those committed to developing graduate courses on reading and its relationship to writing instruction. Appendix B includes resources on the teaching of reading that I have developed and used in professional development workshops for faculty from across the disciplines.

> **Composition needs to continue encouraging studies on the transfer of learning and specifically those that consider the transfer of reading knowledge from first-year composition courses to future courses.**

Following the lead of scholars like Julie Foertsch who argue that the distinction between context-bound knowledge and general knowledge is not so cut and dried, compositionists need to research the most successful methods for helping their students generalize the abstract principles from the reading approaches they learn and practice in first-year composition. Teaching for the transfer of reading knowledge will help supplement the knowledge from composition that students more readily transfer, primarily low-road skills, such as editing. In Benander and Lightner's (2005, 203) study of how students transfer knowledge from general education courses, including composition, they found that students "felt confident transferring low-road skills such as editing, formatting, and citation format," but "many students perceived no connection between their previous English Composition course [Comp I] and the one they were currently attending [Comp 2]." If students are not recognizing connections between these sequenced writing courses then how can we expect them to anticipate connections and transfer reading knowledge from composition to courses in totally different disciplines? The answer, of course, as we know from cognitive and educational psychologists, is that we can't expect this unless we teach for transfer by framing our teaching of reading within a metacognitive framework that consistently helps students abstract general knowledge about reading from the specific reading practices we teach. As we do so, we must monitor the extent to which the transfer of reading knowledge is consistent with what we know about the transfer of writing knowledge. Based on what we discover from comparing the transfer of reading knowledge to the transfer of writing knowledge, we might continue to develop and extend the mindful reading pedagogy outlined in the previous chapter.

> **We must adjust our mindset so that text selection does not over-shadow attention to reading as a practice.**

You will recall that the scholarship from the 1980s and 1990s shifted attention toward *how* students read, yet my study suggests that Patricia Harkin (2005) and Marguerite Helmers (2002), among others, got it right when they pointed out that discussions of reading can quickly morph from questions of *how* to questions of *what*. In the cases I describe below, the question I intended to ask first-year writing instructors—*how* their students read—was misinterpreted as *what* they ask their students to read. Let me explain: I began my interviews with first-year writing instructors by asking them "Can you describe the kinds of reading that students are expected to do in your first-year writing course?" I hoped that the question would get instructors speaking *not* about their text selections (i.e., "kinds of *texts*"), but about how they attended to reading as a practice (i.e., "kinds of *reading*") in their classrooms. Remember that they had already taken the online survey and read the IRB supporting documents that explicitly note that the study's interest is in reading as a *practice* related to writing. Still, instructors responded to my question as if I was asking about text selection, about whether they taught literature or nonfiction. After this happened several times, I changed my inflection to highlight the phrase "*kinds* of *reading*" and made sure to emphasize through my delivery that "reading" was not plural, as in "reading*s*."

Even with this revision and the context that participants were given, the majority of first-year instructors still responded to the question by talking about text selection. Lynda (2012), for example, responded, "The kind of reading that I ask my students to do in my first year comp course would be the kind of reading that they might do if they were picking up a *Time* magazine or a *Discover* or if they were reading something that was in a local newspaper editorial page." Farah (2012) explained, "The first semester uses topical issues to write about [and] the second semester is literature. It is usually a combination of short stories and poetry, and then I and some others are using the option of a novel at the end of the semester." Bailey (2012), too, described the course materials rather than the practices she teaches: "We have two textbooks . . . so they have to read the essays in there." Eventually, I surrendered to these responses altogether and accepted that the first item we would speak about would be text selection and from there I would ask about reading *approaches* they expected students to take as they engaged these texts. Perhaps because we had already talked about text selection, instructors did then comment on the "kinds" of reading I had hoped to get them to speak about first, and the word "approach" seemed to make a difference in reminding instructors that I was interested in practices. The confusion that the first question caused may have been due to a range of problems that Lauer and Asher (1988, 66) note can "afflict questionnaires," including ambiguity and wordiness, but this confusion may also indicate that the place of text selection is at the forefront of the minds even of instructors who are committed to thinking about reading as a practice related to writing. This underscores the uphill battle those interested in reading as a practice will have to face as even this sample of first-year writing instructors who were clearly invested in teaching the practice of reading were quick to focus on textual selection rather than reading as a practice.

Composition's professional organizations should revise their outcomes statements and other documents to first-year writing instruction to better reflect reading's role in the teaching of writing.[1]

Responsible for developing and assessing the writing programs they direct, writing program administrators (WPAs) often use outcomes statements and related documents published by the Conference on College Composition and Communication (CCCC) and Council of Writing Program Administrators (CWPA) to create their own programs and assessment standards. When higher administrators have questions about the writing programs at their institutions, WPAs can point to a set of professionally-sanctioned standards and goals. Looking to these statements for guidance on how to integrate attention to reading in writing programs turns up little help, though. This may mean that WPAs who develop writing programs based on these statements are not likely to create a space for attending to reading in their writing programs. If they are, in fact, inclined to do so on their own, validating this decision to others may be difficult since the field's professional organizations say little about the role reading should play in writing instruction.

Mention of reading is not completely absent from documents developed by CCCC and WPA, but by no means is reading given significant and detailed attention. Moreover, its inclusion is fairly misleading since "reading" is often treated as little more than a placeholder in the triad of goals for first-year writing, which often include critical writing, reading, and thinking. Under the section entitled "Critical Thinking, Reading, and Writing," the WPA Outcomes Statement for First-Year Composition (2008), for example, notes that by the end of first-year composition students should "use writing and reading for inquiry, learning, thinking, and communicating" and in its section on "Rhetorical Knowledge" indicates that students should "understand how genres shape reading and writing." Overall, "reading" appears just a handful of times. This absence is particularly striking in the section on "Processes" that describes the importance of certain practices to effective writing, such as invention, rethinking, revision, and critique.

The CCCC's "Writing Assessment Principles Statement" (revised in 2009) also mentions reading, but does so in a similarly superficial way. The Statement rejects writing assignments that "ask students to form and articulate opinions about some important issue, for instance, without time to reflect, talk to others, read on the subject" while also noting that instructors might ask students to "develop a position on the basis of reading multiple sources." Although the Statement mentions reading, it seems to emphasize the sources, themselves, as opposed to the practice of reading, ultimately neglecting to even allude to what this reading might entail, what it looks like, or how it might be taught.

Another position statement, "Statement of Principles and Standards for the Postsecondary Teaching of Writing," opens with a discussion of CCCC's commitment to supporting the development not just of writers, but of readers: "A democracy demands citizens who can read critically and write clearly and cogently. Developing students' powers as critical readers and writers demands in turn the highest quality of instruction. This quality is the goal to which the Conference on College Composition and Communication (CCCC), the learned society founded in 1949 to serve as the professional association for college teachers of writing, is committed." Unfortunately, though, that ubiquitous notion of critical reading remains undefined here as it often does elsewhere.

Most recently, the WPA and NCTE developed a statement, a "white paper," on writing assessment "meant to help teachers, administrators, and other stakeholders articulate the general positions, values, and assumptions on writing assessment that both the National Council of Teachers of English and the Council of Writing Program Administrators jointly endorse." This statement, like the others, mentions reading's relationship to writing, but does not articulate how one might assess reading in conjunction with one's assessment of students' writing. Instead, it simply notes: "Writing instruction and literacy education at all levels are formal ways in which societies build citizens, and in which citizens develop reading and communication behaviors and competencies in order to participate in various communities. Learning to write better involves engaging in the processes of drafting, reading, and revising; in dialogue, reflections, and formative feedback with peers and teachers; and in formal instruction and imitative activities." Granted, the mention of reading in a discussion of writing assessment practices is promising, but it is not enough.

There is a recently tabled CCCC motion, though, that if reintroduced, has the potential to direct attention to the need to more comprehensively represent reading in these documents.

This motion, which appears in a 2009 CCCC strategic governance document, sets the following as one of CCCC's goals: "CCCC take steps to understand . . . what place does reading have in good writing instruction." Upon following up with the co-authors of the proposal and the NCTE/CCCC liaison who supported the development of this document, I discovered that "some work was done on this motion but it was decided last year [2011] that this was not a priority for the organization to pursue at this time given the organization's current commitments."[2]

The research I have begun and that I am calling for would ultimately allow the CCCCs to articulate more concretely what it means by reading, which activities would fall under this category, and how it imagines reading's relationship to writing. Many of the position statements posted on the CCCC and WPA websites refer to this relationship, but don't address it in depth. Without any specific details about the role of reading in writing instruction, they remain incomplete guides for WPAs own writing programs, as well as ineffective assessment tools. As David Jolliffe (2007, 480) notes, we are left wondering: What are "appropriate reading outcomes for a college writing course?" We might begin to answer this question by pursuing some of the lines of inquiry I lay out in this book.

NOTES

1. The Role of Reading in Composition Studies Special Interest Group, which I co-lead, developed and submitted suggested revisions to the WPA Outcomes Statement for First-Year Composition (2008) that would address reading in more substantial and consistent ways. At press time, the recommendations were being reviewed by the WPA Outcomes Statement Taskforce.
2. A colleague of mine (with a far more intimate understanding of how CCCC's motions come to be) kindly pointed out that motions are not necessarily signals of real disciplinary investments and might more accurately indicate a single person's research interests. Thus, I don't include this information as proof of anything other than the fact that the subject of reading was posited as an important area of inquiry for CCCCs and then discarded as such. As this book details, this has become a pattern within the field.

APPENDIX A
Annotated Bibliography

This annotated bibliography is intended to offer an overview of the discussion concerning the place of reading in writing instruction between 1980 (for reasons detailed in Chapter 4) and the present day. However, it is worth noting that discussions about reading-writing connections have a much longer history than this bibliography suggests. The citations below are best understood as representative of the most contemporary iterations of this discussion.

This bibliography primarily includes publications within the field of composition, as well as English studies, more broadly understood. To a lesser degree, it includes publications from other fields, such as education, when these publications have bearing on post-secondary literacy education and/or have often been cited by compositionists. Paired with this book's works cited list, this bibliography is intended to serve as a resource for those interested in learning about how the subject of reading has been broached in composition. Although not exhaustive, the citations below should, at the very least, point my readers to some of the key scholars who have explored the place of reading in writing instruction and the most salient issues surrounding the subject as these have emerged over the last three decades.

Adler-Kassner, Linda and Heidi Estrem. 2007. "Reading Practices in the Writing Classroom." WPA 31.1–2: 35–47.
  Adler-Kassner and Estrem detail the importance of "considering what we ask students to read, how we ask them to read it, and why" as an "essential aspect of writing program administration" (35). They identify the three most common ways of reading that emerged from studying "artifacts" (40) (e.g., writing heuristics, assignment sheets) from their first-year writing program. To these most common ways, which they list as content-based reading, process-based reading, and

DOI: 10.7330/9780874219609.c008

structure-based reading, they add a fourth element, practice-based reading. This type of reading, they contend, encourages the reader to actively analyze both the "context for her reading and the activity itself" (43). They conclude that identifying the most common purposes for reading in any first-year writing program and deliberately attending to the complex interaction among reader, text, and context can help instructors and writing program administrators demystify the process of reading.

Allen, Ira James. 2012. "Repriviledging Reading: The Negotiation of Uncertainty." Pedagogy, 12.1: 97–120.

Allen describes a study he conducted of tenured faculty members from a range of disciplines in order to better understand their particular reading practices so that he might use these findings to teach his undergraduates how to become more effective, "expert" readers. Allen discovers, though, that faculty members' reading habits are not consistent and that there exists a tension between "how academics do read" and "how we—especially in English departments—talk about wanting our students to read" (99). Specifically, he describes a clash between a "debased, instrumental reading and a better, real reading wherein," simply put, "instrumental readings cares less for the text, real reading more" (99). Conceding that "instrumental" and "real" are no more useful than other terms that have been used to describe similar phenomenon, Allen ultimately concludes that instructors should teach "real reading" as a mode of "negotiating uncertainty" for the range of material and historical-materialist reasons he outlines.

Bartholomae, David. 2005. "The Argument of Reading." In *Writing on the Margins: Essays on Composition and Teaching*, 244–54. New York: Bedford/St. Martin's.

Bartholomae contends that it is worth shifting the discussion away from *what* students in composition courses should read to those surrounding *how* instructors should encourage them to read. He argues that the first-year introductory course should be one in close reading, as defined by the New Critics. He describes the importance of teaching close reading as a form of argumentation and details specific courses (e.g., Hum 6) in which this was done effectively. Ultimately, this emphasis on close reading as argumentation allows students to recognize and argue with those "forms of understanding" they may otherwise take for granted.

Bartholomae, David and Anthony R. Petrosky, eds. 1986. "A Basic Reading and Writing Course for the College Curriculum." In *Facts, Artifacts, and Counterfacts*, 3–43. Portsmouth: Boynton/Cook.

This introduction lays the theoretical foundation for the curriculum and other materials that follow in the book. Bartholomae and Petrosky describe how they came to develop this course in basic reading and writing at the University of Pittsburgh and outline the foundational assumptions upon which it depends. One key assumption is that the "skills approach"—often used in high schools—is problematic for many reasons, including its "fail[ure] to see that comprehending a paragraph in isolation is so very different from comprehending a whole text—in the amount and nature of textual material to be processed and in the nature of a reader's involvement with that material" (12). Bartholomae and Petrosky, instead, represent reading and writing as constructive, conceptual acts and their students as composers "rather than decoders" (15).

Bartholomae, David, Anthony R. Petrosky, and Stacey Waite. 2014. *Ways of Reading*. 10th ed. New York: Bedford/St. Martins.

> This textbook, now in its tenth edition, is intended for use in writing courses that focus on the connections between the interpretive acts of reading and writing. Known for its inclusion of difficult, interdisciplinary texts (e.g., Foucault's "Panopticonism") and challenging assignments, this textbook also includes an extensive, instructive introduction for students that describes the process of reading as a constructive act of meaning making, offers various reading strategies, emphasizes the importance of rereading, and provides an overview of the textbook's assignment sequences and the theory that informs them.

Bazerman, Charles. 1985. "Physicists Reading Physics." *Written Communication* 2.1: 3–23.

> Bazerman reports his findings from a study in which he observes and interviews physicists reading. Bazerman finds that these processes are "permeated with individual purposes and schema" (3). These schema include both "consensual knowledge about the phenomena being discussed" and "perceptions as to the most promising lines of current work" (3). Ultimately, Bazerman concludes that schema and purposes inform how these physicists read and thus help account for how complex and varied their reading processes are.

Bazerman, Charles. 1980. "A Relationship between Reading and Writing: The Conversation Model." *College English* 41.6: 656–661.

> Bazerman argues against the turn in composition at this time toward expressivist ways of thinking about writing that often "emphasize the writer's original voice, which has its source in an independent self" (657). He contends, instead, that composition needs to focus on the contexts in which people write. This remedy involves teaching students to write in a conversational context that compels them to experience the connections between reading and writing since "intelligent response beings *with accurate understanding of prior comments*, not just of the facts and ideas stated, but of what the other writer was trying to achieve" (658, emphasis in original). The model of written conversation that he calls for seeks to expand students' abilities to write in a range of contexts, including those outside of the academy.

Bean, John C, ed. 2001. "Helping Students Read Difficult Texts." In *Engaging Ideas*, 133–148. San Francisco: Jossey-Bass.

> Bean contends that in order to help students read more deeply instructors need to be aware of the obstacles that students face when

they read. He outlines 10 of these obstacles and then offers strategies for dealing with them in order to make students "better readers" (133).

Berthoff, Ann E. 1981. *Forming/Thinking/Writing*. Montclair, N.J.: Boynton/Cook.

Berthoff lays out her theory of reading and writing, which locates both as acts of composing meaning. Berthoff describes how this theory informs her teaching of reading and writing and she includes various assignments, such as the dialectical notebook that support her teaching.

Berthoff, Ann E. 1981. *The Making of Meaning: Metaphors, Models, and Maxims for Writing Teachers*. Montclair, N. J.: Boynton/Cook.

This book is a collection of talks and articles Berthoff wrote in the 1970s and early 1980s and is intended for use by teachers at all levels of the curriculum (K-post-secondary schools), as well as researchers. Throughout this collection, Berthoff speaks out against the conception of reading and writing as skills that can be compartmentalized and taught, and instead argues for the conception of reading and writing as meaning-making acts that can only effectively be taught within this interpretive framework.

Bialostosky, Don. 2006. "Should College English Be Close Reading?" *College English* 69: 111–116.

In this essay, Bialostosky details the problems with the ubiquity of the term "close reading" and argues that this term often goes undefined in scholarship and teaching precisely because it has become so commonplace. This is problematic, Bialostosky contends, because it covers over the need to precisely define the reading practices instructors value and would like to teach their students. Bialostosky calls for more attention to these specific practices and suggests that those in English studies stop relying on this concept of close reading. Doing so, he argues, will open up the space to attend to those practices for which this "umbrella term" often stands in.

Bishop, Wendy. 1997. "Reading, Stealing, and Writing like a Writer." In *Elements of Alternate Style: Essays on Writing and Revision*, edited by Wendy Bishop, 119–130. Portsmouth, NH: Boynton/Cook.

Bishop encourages students to pay attention to the sentences they come across in order to notice how "varied and flexible" (121) sentences can be. She argues for the importance not of memorizing rules governing the ways to construct sentences, but, instead, she describes the practice of "stealing" (128) those techniques one admires in other people's sentences. "Tinkering" (129) and playing with sentences, she contends, can help students better understand how sentences work.

Blau, Sheridan. 2003. *The Literature Workshop*. Portsmouth, N. H.: Heinemann.

In this book, Blau describes his approach to teaching introductory literature courses to post-secondary students. He details what he calls "the literature workshop" and includes transcripts of these workshops, ways to adapt his approach, as well as other helpful resources for instructors. The goal of these workshops is to help students become autonomous, disciplined readers and to do so Blau encourages the use of metacognitive and reflective exercises. In his own reflections on these workshops, Blau draws out various principles of reading and discusses these in terms of published scholarship on reading, including the work of Louise Rosenblatt, Robert Scholes, and Robert Tierney.

Brandt, Deborah. 1994. "Remembering Writing, Remembering Reading." *College Composition and Communication* 45.4: 459–79.

Brandt describes interviews with 40 people wherein she asks them to reflect on their experiences with reading and writing. Her goal is to explore "literacy learning as it has occurred across the twentieth century." She finds that the people she interviews associate reading far more often with "sensual and emotional pleasure" while they associate writing with "the pain and isolation it was meant to assuage."

Brent, Doug. 1992. *Reading as Rhetorical Invention.* Urbana, IL: NCTE.

Brent argues that reading as a practice has been largely under-theorized and explored. He defines reading according to its similarities to writing, describing it as epistemic and dependent on social and cognitive processes. Ultimately, he calls for more attention to the reader (i.e., the "consumer") in rhetorical analyses rather than just the writer (i.e., the "producer") and models what this work might look like as he describes rhetoric's need for a theory of reading.

Brost, Brian D. and Karen A. Bradley. 2006. "Student Compliance with Assigned Reading: A Case Study." *Journal of Scholarship of Teaching and Learning* 6.2: 101–111.

Challenging more common approaches to the issue of student compliance with assigned reading, which are almost exclusively student-centered, this piece considers the faculty's role in this noncompliance. Specifically, this article details how faculty members often (unknowingly) promote the apathy their students display. Brost and Bradley ultimately offer suggestions for how faculty might more productively conceive of and integrate reading into their courses.

Bunn, Mike. 2011. "How to Read like a Writer." *Writing Spaces: Readings on Writing, Volume* 2, 71–86. Anderson, South Carolina: Parlor Press.

As do Wendy Bishop, Charles Moran, Nancy Walker, and Stuart Greene (see citations), Bunn emphasizes the importance of helping students recognize the connections between the processes of reading and writing by detailing the "reading like a writer" strategy that connects these practices. The essay, which is addressed to students, encourages them to pay attention to the writing techniques that characterize the reading they complete in order to imagine how they might integrate these techniques into their own writing. In this piece, unlike the others, Bunn offers a systematic, step-by-step, explanation of how students can begin to read like writers.

Bunn, Michael. 2013. "Motivation and Connection: Teaching Reading (and Writing) in the Composition Classroom." *College Composition and Communication* 64: 496–516.

> Drawing on a study he conducted at the University of Michigan, Bunn addresses the extent to which first-year composition instructors teach reading-writing connections in their courses. He also considers related issues, including student motivation and the teaching of model texts. Ultimately, he argues that using model texts as a means to fore-grounding reading-writing connections can go a long way toward moti-vating students to complete reading for their writing courses.

Bunn, Michael. 2011. "Reading Visual Rhetoric in Composition Courses: Adopting an Approach that Helps Students Produce Their Own Visual Discourse." *Reader* 61: 87–103.

> In this essay, Bunn explores the concept of visual rhetoric in order to imagine how it might be defined and taught in college composition courses. One of the major goals of such work is to help students see the connections between the visual texts they read and those texts they will produce, texts they must "design" through the use of rhetorical features. Bunn details the assignments he uses to teach visual rhetorical and how these support students' writing.

Bunn, Michael Thomson. 2010. "Reconceptualizing the Role of Reading in Composition Studies." Diss. University of Michigan. http://deepblue.lib.umich.edu/handle/2027.42/77796

> In this doctoral dissertation, Bunn identifies and explores reasons why the field of composition has largely neglected reading as a subject of inquiry. The dissertation presents a topography of reading approach-es culled from the field's professional discourse, as well as a quantita-tive study of how reading figures into the teaching of first-year composi-tion at the University of Michigan. He "compares how these instructors define and describe various reading approaches with the definitions and descriptions found in scholarship, thus offering a more complete picture of how reading is theorized and taught in first-year writing courses." He found that "instructor data reinforces how inexact the definitions for these reading approaches are and how this imprecision can make it difficult to teach reading effectively" (vi). Bunn concludes with recommendations for effectively integrating attention to reading in first-year composition courses.

Carillo, Ellen C. 2009. "Making Reading Visible in the Classroom." *Currents in Teaching and Learning*.1.2: 37–41.

> Carillo explores the difficulties that characterize the teaching of reading in the undergraduate classroom. She details a specific assign-ment, the passage-based paper (PBP), that she has found useful in making students' reading visible so that she can offer support and feedback on their reading as instructors do on students' writing. Carillo concludes by detailing the uses of this assignment beyond English and the humanities.

Downs, Doug. 2010. "Teaching First-Year Writers to Use Texts: Scholarly Readings in Writing-about-Writing in First-Year Comp." *Reader* 60: 19–50.

> Downs explores the place of reading instruction in general education courses and particularly first-year composition courses. He describes the potential conflict inherent in the notion that reading (like writing) is context-bound and embedded in community practices while instruction in general education courses like first-year writing is supposed to offer just that, general instruction. With this conflict in mind, he goes on to detail how he effectively incorporates scholarly readings in his first-year "writing about writing" (WAW) courses.

Elbow, Peter. 1993. "The War between Reading and Writing—and How to End It." *Rhetoric Review.* 12.1: 5–24.

> Elbow's piece is divided into four sections that explore the following: sites of conflict between reading and writing; how reading is privileged over writing; benefits of ending this privilege; and ways to end the war and create a more productive interaction between reading and writing. Ultimately, Elbow argues for the importance of attending to reading and writing in ways that allow both processes to "reinforce each other as equals." To this end, he offers specific teaching practices, activities, and necessary curricular changes.

Ettari, Gary and Heather C. Easterling. 2002. "Reading (and) the Profession." *Reader* 47: 9–37.

> Ettari and Easterling argue that "one of the difficulties that is evident at [their] institution and perhaps others as well, is the underexamined role of reading and its practice in the different courses we teach" (10). They lament the lack of attention to reading in graduate programs even though reading is "one of the central activities" (10) in English studies. They contend that those in the field should "more clearly articulate not only the different kinds of reading we demand from our students but also how student reading and student writing inform and contribute to one another" or we risk "oversimplifying a complex and important issue," thereby "compromising both our students' education and our own as professionals" (20).

Goldschmidt, Mary. 2010. "Marginalia: Teaching Texts, Teaching Readers, Teaching Writers." *Reader* 60: 51–69.

> Goldschmidt describes her use of "extensive marginal notations" to foster "transferrable skills" (53). Rather than having students use the more traditional ways of marking a text, such as underlining, highlighting, bracketing, and so on, Goldschmidt asks students to instead "write out their thoughts about why they would have marked the passage" (60). Students then share their responses with the class. From there, students take inventory of their notes by applying Goldschmidt's marginalia checklist that allows them to label their marginal notes in terms of the function each performs (e.g., it identifies the main point, comments on the author's methodology, reacts emotionally). Goldschmidt contends that this and other marginalia activities compel students to

self-monitor and hone their metacognitive abilities while allowing her to teach texts, readers, and writers simultaneously.

Goen, Sugie and Helen Gillotte-Tropp. 2003. "Integrated Reading and Writing: A Response to the Basic Writing 'Crisis.'" *Journal of Basic Writing* 22.2: 90–113.

Goen and Gillotte-Tropp describe the development of a program at San Francisco State University that integrates reading and writing rather than treating them separately as do most developmental literacy programs. The goal of the program and its curriculum is to take advantage of the connections between the practices of reading and writing. Goen and Gillotte-Tropp conclude by describing their efforts to assess this integrated curriculum, which ultimately show that students benefited from this approach and having completed the program were prepared to enter mainstream courses.

Goodman, Kenneth. 1996. *On Reading.* Portsmouth, NH: Heinemann.

Goodman's work on reading informs a great deal of modern scholarship on reading. In this text, he provides an in-depth account of the theories he developed about reading, which date back to the 1970s. He describes reading as a "psycholinguistic guessing game" (7) that does not involve recognizing letters and words, but constructing meaning. He explains the complex process of constructing meaning as a reader, which involves predicting what comes next in a text. He also introduces the idea of miscue analysis that provides instructors insight into how and why students "misread."

Greene, Stuart. 1993. "Exploring the Relationship between Authorship and Reading." In *Hearing Ourselves Think,* edited by Ann Penrose and Barbara Sitko, 33–51. New York: Oxford University Press.

Greene explores the connection between reading and authorship by describing a pedagogy that locates students as authors who read the writing of others with an eye toward the rhetorical techniques they use so that they may experiment with them in their own writing. Greene contends that as students mine these texts they "recognize that the choices and decisions they make as writers vary according to the social context in which they write."

Haas, Christina. 1990. "Beyond 'Just the Facts': Reading as Rhetorical Action." In *Hearing Ourselves Think: Cognitive Research in the College Writing Classroom,* edited by Ann M. Penrose and Barbara M. Sitho, 19–32. Oxford: Oxford University Press.

Working from a social-constructivist perspective, Haas expands upon her earlier study with Flower (see citation just below) by considering to what extent rhetorical context influences readers' comprehension and use of reading strategies. She demonstrates that reading is a "constructive, rhetorical, decision-making activity," (29) and includes a series of classroom activities and assignments that have the potential to "enrich students' understanding and practices of reading" (20).

Haas, Christina and Linda Flower. 1988. "Rhetorical Reading Strategies and the Construction of Meaning." *College Composition and Communication* 39.2: 167–183.

    Haas and Flower describe a reading study they conducted wherein they used a think-aloud protocol to determine the strategies that experienced (i.e., graduate students) and less experienced (i.e., under-graduates) use when reading. Haas and Flower found that graduate students used "rhetorical" reading strategies to make sense of the text before them and undergraduates used these strategies rarely as they largely understood reading as information-exchange. These findings lead them to argue that undergraduate instructors need to help students move beyond this information-exchange view to a "more complex rhetorical model" (182) of reading (and writing). Haas and Flower ultimately describe the importance of instructors teaching undergraduate rhetorical reading strategies and focusing on "teaching readers" rather than "teaching texts" (169).

Haswell, Richard, et al. 1999. "Context and Rhetorical Reading Strategies: Haas and Flower (1988) Revisited." *Written Communication* 16.3: 3–27.

    Haswell et al. replicate Haas and Flower's 1988 reading study (see citation just above) to determine to what extent the content of the text that undergraduate students read affected the results. Whereas Haas and Flower found that graduate students used "rhetorical" reading strategies to make sense of the text before them and undergraduates used these strategies rarely, Haswell et al. found that with a text on a more familiar topic, undergraduates did, in fact, read rhetorically far more often. The piece concludes with an overview of the implications of this replication for teachers and researchers.

Harkin, Patricia. 2005. "The Reception of Reader-Response Theory." *College Composition and Communication* 56.3: 410–425.

    This essay explores the place of reader-response theory in English studies. Taking a historical approach, Harkin describes reader-response theory as belonging to two movements, namely the 1970s theory boom, which she positions as elitist, and the political movements of the 1960s and 1970s, which she represents as populist. She argues that if "the theory boom was to remain elitist, it had to deauthorize reader-response" while "if reader-response was to remain populist, it had to consent to and participate in that deauthorization" (410). She ultimately contends that reader-response theory, along with attention to reading, all but disappeared in English studies during the last decade of the twentieth century because it was populist. Harkin concludes by calling for the recuperation of the scholarship on reading.

Helmers, Marguerite, ed. 2002. *Intertexts: Reading Pedagogy in College Writing Classrooms.* Mahwah, NJ: Lawrence Erlbaum Associates, Inc.

    This anthology consists of chapters that address and often rethink the separation of reading from writing. The contributors, which include Mariolina Rizzi Salvatori, Kathleen McCormick, Patricia Harkin, and James J. Sosnoski, take a range of theoretical approaches

to this issue and explore it within various frameworks including cultural
studies, reader response theory, electronic literacy, creative writing,
and literary criticism. Helmers opens the anthology with an introduction that defines reading as a process far more complex than merely
absorbing or consuming a text. In this introduction she also addresses
omissions that the reader is likely to notice in the anthology, including
attention to assessment, as well as gender- and class-inflected theories
of reading.

Henry, Jeanne. 2009. "Cultivating Reading Workshop: New Theory into Practice." *Open Words* 3.1: 62–74.

Henry revisits her reading workshop approach, detailed in her
1995 book, in order to revise her understanding and representation
of her students. Whereas Henry calls her students "non readers" and
"reluctant readers" in this earlier work, she uses this piece to describe
how she has come to "revalue" her students as readers and find ways to
encourage students' valuing of themselves as readers (64). She details
her development of classroom activities that draw attention to the ways
students have already managed and even found pleasure in literacy
experiences (e.g., through reading religious texts and community news-
letters). These activities encourage students to cultivate more positive
associations with reading.

Horner, Winifred Bryan, ed. 1983. *Composition and Literature: Bridging the Gap.*
Chicago: University of Chicago Press.

This anthology brings together essays by scholars in both composition and literature in order to explore the gap between these two fields
and the artificial separation this creates between the teaching of writing and the teaching of reading. Contributors include, among others,
J. Hillis Miller, Richard Lanham, Wayne Booth, Walter Ong, Elaine
P. Maimon, Robert Scholes, E. D. Hirsch, and Edward P. J. Corbett.
Horner introduces the collection by providing historical context and
framing the anthology as an attempt by scholars from composition
and literature to "join forces" in order to "find the strength and the
resources to forge new directions in the discipline [of English]" (8).

Horning, Alice S. 1987. "The Trouble with Reading is the Trouble with
Writing." *Journal of Basic Writing* 6.1: 36–47.

Horning presents two case studies that tentatively support her
hypothesis that "specific syntactic and semantic difficulties in writing
are related to reading problems in syntax and comprehension among
basic writers" (36). After describing her methodology and the two case
studies, she explores the implications of her findings for both theory
and practice.

Horning, Alice S. 2007. "Reading across the Curriculum as the Key to Student
Success." *Across the Disciplines* 4. http://wac.colostate.edu/atd/articles
/horning2007.cfm.

Horning argues that just as writing across the curriculum programs
have focused instructors' attention on teaching writing, *reading* across

the curriculum programs have the potential to do the same for reading. She notes that "it seems clear that a refocused emphasis on reading as the process of getting meaning from print to be used for analysis, synthesis and evaluation, in the context of critical literacy across the curriculum could potentially address the difficulties of students, the goals of teachers and the needs of the nation for an educated, informed, fully participatory democratic population." She goes on to list and describe four specific strategies that support this goal.

Horning, Alice S. 2013. *Reading, Writing, and Digitizing Literacy in the Electronic Age*. Cambridge Scholars Press.

In this book, Horning locates reading, writing, and digitizing as processes of constructing meaning. She incorporates research on how both novice and expert readers engage with texts and argues for the importance of teaching students how to become "meta-readers" (1). To this end, she offers concrete strategies for helping students reach this goal.

Horning, Alice and Elizabeth Kraemer, eds. 2013. *Reconnecting Reading and Writing*. Parlor Press.

This collection includes a range of perspectives on why reading should be reunited with writing in secondary and post-secondary classrooms. Authors address what this unification would mean for different student populations, including second language learners and "basic" writers, as well as how attention to reading practices in writing instruction would affect the implementation of Common Core Standards.

Huffman, Debrah. 2010. "Towards Modes of Reading in Composition." *Reader* 60: 162–188.

Huffman offers a detailed study of how introductory composition textbooks teach (both explicitly and implicitly) college students to read. She considers five, "popular" (165) textbooks that are in their fifth or later editions. Conceding that a textbook study alone does not provide access to how the textbooks are actually used, she concludes by noting that while these textbooks tend to teach only "interpretation," (181) composition instructors need to help their students imagine other ways of and reasons for reading.

Irwin, Judith W. and Mary Anne Doyle, eds. 1992. *Reading/Writing Connections: Learning from Research*. Newark, DE: International Reading Association.

This book includes chapters that draw on research studies to answer questions about how the processes of reading and writing interact and what instructors can do to maximize the connections between reading and writing in their classrooms. The contributors, which include Judith Langer, Jill Fitzgerald, Peter Smagorinksy, and Robert Tierney, draw on a range of research methodologies, including ethnographic studies, protocol analyses, and participant-observer studies. The final section of the collection includes a discussion of future paths for research, as well as an overview of all of the research conducted on reading/writing connections between 1900 and 1984. The members of the International Reading Association read and evaluated this research in order to develop a bibliography of the "best research" in the field, which is also included.

Iser, Wolfgang. 1978. *The Act of Reading: A Theory of Aesthetic Response.* Baltimore: Johns Hopkins University Press.

Iser explores the relationship between the reader and text by "bring[ing] to light the elementary operations which the text activates within the reader," (ix) as well as the characteristics of that interaction. He calls this response "aesthetic" because it "brings into play the imaginative and perceptive faculties of the reader." Iser analyzes the act of reading primarily through a phenomenological frame, drawing heavily on the theories he puts forth in his earlier work, *The Implied Reader.*

Jolliffe, David A. 2007. "Learning to Read as Continuing Education." *College Composition and Communication* 58.3: 470–494.

In this review essay of *Subjects Matter: Every Teacher's Guide to Content-Area Reading* by Harvey Daniels and Steven Zemelman; *Intertexts: Reading Pedagogy in College Writing Classrooms* by Marguerite Helmers; *Do I Really Have to Teach Reading? Content Comprehension, grades 6–12* by Cris Tovani; and *Teaching Literature as Reflective Practice* by Kathleen Blake Yancey, Jolliffe explores how these texts speak to ways that secondary and post-secondary instructors might actively and productively address reading in their teaching, research, and scholarship. He opens by considering how instructors might build a "challenging, serviceable, teachable model of reading for their courses" and addresses the "stumbling blocks conceptual, attitudinal, and pragmatic that impede instructors' and students' giving critical reading its due in college composition courses" (472). In reviewing the books he focuses on their suggestions for how the "best college instructors of composition and other fields can think about themselves as teachers of reading" (472). Jolliffe's goal is to "convince readers that college composition instruction can capitalize on (and improve) students' high school reading experiences if instructors and program administrators think carefully about where their students are starting as readers, where they want them to get by the end of the course" (472).

Jolliffe, David A. 2003. "Who is Teaching Composition Students to Read and How Are They Doing It?" *Composition Studies* 31.1: 127–142.

In this review essay of Ellin Oliver Keene and Susan Zimmerman's *Mosaic of Thought: Teaching Comprehension in a Reader's Workshop* and Cris Tovani's *I Read It, but I Don't Get it: Comprehension Strategies for Adolescents,* Jolliffe uses these texts, which have been adopted as the basis of in-service professional development programs on reading for teachers in American school districts, to imagine how they might inform the teaching of college composition. His focus, in particular, is on "critical reading" and how (and to what extent) critical reading is being taught in high schools and first-year composition courses.

Jolliffe, David A. and Allison Harl. 2008. "Studying the 'Reading Transition' from High School to College: What Are Our Students Reading and Why?" *College English* 70.6: 599–617.

    Jolliffe and Harl describe a study they conducted at their institution, the University of Arkansas, in order to discover how their first-year students taking composition "perceived and effected the transition from high school to college as readers" (600). They studied students' reading habits by having students self-report and keep reading journals for two weeks. Joliffe and Harl concluded that students were passionate about reading, but not about the reading they were doing for their classes. While they were able to draw "text-to-self" connections they struggled drawing "text-to-text" and "text-to-world" connections (612–13). The piece ends with recommendations for motivating students to read in writing courses.

Keller, Daniel. 2013. *Chasing Literacy: Reading and Writing in an Age of Acceleration.* Logan: Utah State University Press.

    In this book, Keller explores the importance of teaching reading and writing alongside each other. He takes a social-cultural approach to thinking about how one constructs meaning from texts and multimodal and digital texts, in particular. Drawing on several case studies wherein Keller observes students engaging in different kinds of reading (print-based and digital) both at home and at school, Keller argues for the importance of preparing both instructors and students for "the expansion of genres and media" (4). He concludes by outlining a reading pedagogy that draws on his conclusions from his case studies, as well as other relevant research and scholarship.

Kelemen, Erick. 2011. "Critical Editing and Close Reading in the Undergraduate Classroom." *Pedagogy* 12.1: 121–138.

    Kelemen argues for teaching undergraduates how to employ textual criticism. He focuses, specifically, on teaching students scholarly editing practices, which allows students to participate in the questions that the field of manuscript studies raises, including those surrounding the definition of an author, the work, and canons. Kelemen links the process of editing to close reading, which serves as the framework for editing assignments. This approach to editing, Kelemen contends, allows students to experience editing as an interpretive act. Moreover, students experience how many decisions go into editing, which has the potential to support their work as peer editors. Kelemen concludes by emphasizing that students may not be the best scholarly editors, but that their engagement in the *process* of doing so is where the value of this work resides.

Lindemann, Erika. 1993. "Freshman Composition: No Place for Literature." *College English* 55.3: 311–16.

    One half of what has been called the "Lindemann-Tate debate," Lindemann argues that imaginative literature such as poetry, drama, and fiction has no place within the first-year composition course, recommending, instead, that instructors ask students to read non-literary texts that better represent the scholarly conversations students will likely be asked to enter throughout their academic careers. Lindemann contends that although instructors may be more comfortable teaching literature, this takes time away from working on students' writing, the focus of the course. In addition to text selection she focuses on the importance of attending to reading practices, and ultimately recommends disciplinary-specific writing courses.

Linkon, Sherry. 2005. "The Reader's Apprentice: Making Critical Cultural Reading Visible." *Pedagogy* 5.2: 247–273.
      Linkon argues that if instructors want students to develop sophisticated reading, researching, and analytical abilities, instructors must "employ more strategic, deliberate methods of teaching" (248). She concedes that these processes cannot be described as a series of steps, but that instructors can teach students the "qualities and common practices involved in expert reading" (251). Linkon outlines these features and describes how she teaches them in her classroom, as well as how she seeks to debunk some of the assumptions students have about research and reading.

Manarin, Karen. 2012. "Reading Value: Student Choice in Reading Strategies." *Pedagogy* 12. 2: 281–297.
      This essay is based on a 2009 research project Manarin conducted wherein she studied how students in two sections of a course on critical writing and reading read a range of nonfiction texts. Her goal was to "better understand what reading strategies students select when dealing with assigned texts" (282). In addition to describing her findings, she offers an overview of educational research on reading, how her study affected her own teaching and course design, and how her findings might inform the development of effective ways to teach reading and writing.

McCormick, Kathleen. 1994. *The Culture of Reading / The Teaching of English.* Manchester, England: Manchester University Press.
      McCormick's goal in this book is to move beyond theory in order to offer accounts of reading—some ideological, some historical, some institutional, and some classroom-based—in order to intervene in discussions about the revision of curricula in Britain and America. She explores expressivist, cognitive, and social cultural approaches to reading in order to expose the dynamic nature of the relationship among text, reader, and context in each.

Middleton, Holly. 2012. "Recognizing Acts of Reading: Creating Reading Outcomes and Assessments for Writing." *WPA* 36.1: 11–31.
      Drawing on the results of a reading study she conducted at her university, Middleton argues that developing and aligning reading and writing outcomes for writing programs is a crucial step toward a more comprehensive treatment in the field of composition of the relationship between reading and writing. Particularly interested in students' reading comprehension, Middleton also calls for more research on the relationship between reading and writing.

Moran, Charles. 1990. "Reading like a Writer." In *Vital Signs 1*, edited by James L. Collins, 60–69. Portsmouth, NH: Boynton/Cook.

> Moran sets out to answer two questions in this piece: "Why do we teach literature?" and "How shall we teach literature?" Moran underscores the problematic separation of reading from writing and describes the importance of "reading like a writer" for teaching students how to better understand the decisions that writers make.

Morrow, Nancy. 1997. "The Role of Reading in the Composition Classroom." *JAC* 17.3: 453–472.

> Morrow contends that instead of focusing on textual selection in discussions about reading in writing courses, teacher-scholars instead should ask: "Why do we read in composition classes?" (453). She claims that "by focusing more carefully on what happens when students read, we can make more astute choices about both course design and text selection" (453). Her essay goes on to offer a detailed summary of some of the debates that have characterized the field of English studies, most of which revolve around which texts to teach, and she concludes with a detailed list of various models of reading (e.g., reading for genre conventions, reading for ambiguity) intended to help instructors expose and reflect on how they expect their students to read.

Murphy, James. 1982. "Rhetorical History as a Guide to Salvation of American Reading and Writing: A Plea for Curricular Courage." In *The Rhetorical Tradition and Modern Writing*, edited by James Murphy, 3–12. New York: MLA.

> Murphy outlines the splintering of English departments into two separate camps in which one set of professors (i.e., those of literature) teach reading and the other set (i.e., composition instructors) teach writing. This "deeply rooted division," a result of specialized writing courses, he contends, is "ridiculous" and counterproductive to the work of English (3).

Murray, Heather. 1991. "Close Reading, Closed Writing." *College English* 53.2: 195–208.

> Murray points out that despite English studies' theoretical position against it, close reading "persists in our practices, and especially pedagogic ones" (195). The goal of her essay is to explore the implications of the "institutionalization and intractability" (195) of close reading and what this ultimately means for English studies and its students.

Nelson, Nancy. 1998. "Reading and Writing Contextualized." In *The Reading-Writing Connection*, edited by Nancy Nelson and Robert C. Calfee, 266–285. Chicago, IL: University of Chicago Press.

> A publication of the National Society of Education, this volume is divided into four sections that address, in varying ways, how reading and writing have been separated in American schools. The first section, written by the book's editors, explores this issue within a historical framework that traces this practice in schools back to colonial times. The second section includes essays that explore the relationship between authors and readers. The third section considers reading with-

in a classroom context and includes essays concerning how teachers read and respond to student texts. The final section places reading in a disciplinary context by addressing the value of writing about literature.

Newell, George E., et al. 2011. "Teaching and Learning Argumentative Reading and Writing: A Review of Research." *Reading Research Quarterly* 46.3: 273–304.

Newell et al. offer an overview of empirical research conducted on the teaching and learning of argumentative writing and reading practices in K–12 and college writing classrooms, primarily from cognitive and social research perspectives. Newell et al. explore the assumptions that inform each research perspective, as well as their instructional consequences. Ultimately, they argue for additional research on teaching and learning argumentative reading and writing, research that brings together cognitive and social research perspectives.

Newkirk, Thomas, ed. 1986. *Only Connect: Uniting Reading and Writing.* Montclair, NJ: Boynton/Cook.

This collection of papers drawn from talks given at a conference held at the University of New Hampshire in October, 1984 includes contributions from Richard Ohmann, Robert J. Connors, David Bartholomae, Ann E. Berthoff, Judith Goleman, Gary Lindberg, Louise Z. Smith, Charles Moran, Donald M. Murray, and Paul Mariani. These contributors take different approaches to considering the relationship between reading and writing, some exploring it through a historical perspective, others addressing reading and writing within a reader-response and related literary studies frameworks, and others still focusing on classroom issues.

Petersen, Bruce T., ed. 1986. *Convergences: Transactions in Reading and Writing.* Urbana, IL: NCTE.

This collection includes essays written by key players in discussions about reading-writing connections, including Louise Rosenblatt, Robert J. Tierney, David Bleich, and Joseph Comprone. The essays published in this collection represent reading as a transactive process and explore what this conception of reading means for researchers and classroom teachers (at all levels of the curriculum) alike.

Petrosky, Anthony. 1982. "From Story to Essay: From Reading to Writing." *College Composition and Communication* 33: 19–37.

Petrosky argues that reading is as much a process of constructing meaning as writing. He uses reading research from cognitive psychology, among other fields, to support his argument and uses student texts to show how students who write about their reading ultimately better understand the texts.

Qualley, Donna. 2010. "Disciplinary Ways of Teaching Reading in English." *Reader* 60: 4–17.

Qualley introduces this issue of *Reader*, which she guest edits, by raising a series of questions about the teaching of reading that she says necessarily apply to everyone in the field of English since students in all English classes are expected to read. The contributors to this issue

tackle these questions by drawing on a range of "disciplinary and expe-
riential perspectives," (5) including literature, first-year composition,
non-fiction memoir writing, and English education.

Qualley, Donna.1997. *Turns of Thought.* Portsmouth, NH: Boynton/Cook.

> Qualley argues for the teaching of writing and reading as "essayistic"
> enterprises that are tentative and dialogic in nature. She demonstrates
> through a range of classroom-based examples how she teaches reading
> and writing in this way that demands that students consistently return
> to their reading and writing experiences in order to rethink and revise
> them in reflexive ways. Qualley contends that this type of reflexive
> essayistic reading and writing has the potential to transform students'
> understandings of texts, themselves, and the world around them.

Qualley, Donna.1993. "Using Reading in the Writing Classroom." In *Nuts and
Bolts: A Practical Guide to Teaching College Composition,* edited by Thomas
Newkirk, 101–128. Portsmouth, NH: Boynton/Cook.

> This chapter describes Qualley's approach to integrating reading
> into her first-year writing courses. She details assignments and class-
> room activities (e.g., the double-entry notebook, reading conferences)
> that help students understand, among other things, that reading and
> writing are related processes, that people read differently, and that
> reading involves making connections. Ultimately her goal is to "demys-
> tify" (115) the reading process by drawing students' attention to how—
> through reading—they make meaning from the texts they encounter.

Rosenblatt, Louise. 2005. *Making Meaning with Texts: Selected Essays.* Portsmouth,
NH: Heinemann.

> This group of essays includes some of Rosenblatt's most seminal
> essays, dating back to 1938, on the relationship between the reader and
> the text. She divides the essays into what she calls two "major interrelat-
> ed emphases: Theory and Practice" (xi). These essays detail her invest-
> ment in privileging not the text itself, but the reader and the reading
> experience, which she calls "transactional" (x). The collection also
> includes a preface to readers written by Rosenblatt, as well as a 1999
> interview with her after she had been awarded the NCTE's Outstanding
> Educator in the Language Arts award.

Salvatori, Mariolina Rizzi.1996. "The Argument of Reading in the Teaching
of Composition." In *Argument Revisited: Argument Redefined,* edited by B.
Emmel, P. Resch, and D. Tenney, 181–190. Sage Publications.

> Salvatori explores the importance of incorporating attention to
> reading in the writing classroom, particularly as a means to teach argu-
> mentative writing. She separates herself from other scholars who are
> interested in whether reading should be used in composition, describ-
> ing her investment, instead, in "*which kind of reading* gets to be theorized
> and practiced" (185, emphasis in original). Her piece takes up the fol-
> lowing three questions: "1) Which theories of reading are better suited
> to teaching reading and writing as connected activities? 2) What is the
> theoretical justification for privileging that interconnectedness? 3) How
> can one teach that interconnectedness?" (185–92.)

Salvatori, Mariolina Rizzi. 1996. "Conversations with Texts: Reading in the Teaching of Composition." *College English* 58.4: 440–454.

Salvatori contends that more important than thinking about which texts students read in composition courses is the type of reading instructors should encourage. She contends that recursive reading, which depends upon self-monitoring practices, offers students opportunities to become aware of the relationship among reading, writing, and thinking.

Salvatori, Mariolina Rizzi. 1983. "Reading and Writing a Text: Correlations between Reading and Writing Patterns." *College English* 45.7: 656–666.

Salvatori explains the danger in artificially separating the practices of reading and writing as represented by the fields of literature and composition. She argues that because language skills are, in fact, related it is worthwhile to spend time considering how to teach composition in ways that take advantage of this connection. Using the scholarship of David Bartholomae, Ann E. Berthoff, and Wolfgang Iser, Salvatori studies one student's development as a reader and writer ultimately concluding that this student may not have made the strides she did had she been in a composition course in which reading was not given as much attention as writing.

Salvatori, Mariolina Rizzi and Patricia Donahue. 2005. *The Elements (and Pleasures) of Difficulty.* New York: Longman.

This textbook intended for students in English studies is centered on the concept of difficulty. By engaging with texts that challenge students (e.g., through their complex ideas, strange content, ambiguities, confusing language), this textbook seeks to encourage students to confront difficulty as a means to developing intellectually, recognizing what they already know, and becoming confident in their reading and writing abilities. The textbook contains a range of readings, including poetry, prose narratives, and personal essays that are accompanied by assignments that foster active reading practices within metacognitive frameworks. The textbook includes an introduction to instructors that explains the pedagogy of difficulty, as well as an introduction addressed to students that describes, in depth, this concept of difficulty. Among other materials, the appendices contain strategies to help students deal with difficulty.

Salvatori, Mariolina Rizzi and Patricia Donahue. 2012. "Stories about Reading: Appearance, Disappearance, Morphing, and Revival." *College English* 75.2: 199–217.

Inspired by the revival of interest in reading within composition, Salvatori and Donahue trace the rise and fall of the discipline's investment in studying and teaching reading. Focusing on the rise of reader-response theory, the ways the discipline has sought to define itself, the "misnamed" Lindemann-Tate debate, and the disappearance for seventeen years of reading as a potential topic for panels and individual presentations at the CCCCs annual convention, Salvatori and Donahue argue that because reading is taken for granted, it has ceased to be at the center of the field's discussions as it once was in the 1980s and early 1990s. Salvatori and Donahue imagine their essay as a step toward underscoring the importance of attending overtly and deliberately to questions surrounding the teaching of and research on reading and suggest avenues for further inquiry about reading's place in writing instruction.

Scholes, Robert. 2002. "The Transition to College Reading." *Pedagogy* 2.2: 165–172.

Scholes describes the difficulty of attending to reading in the college classroom since students' reading is not visible in the same way that their writing is. Because instructors cannot see how students read they cannot offer feedback on their reading practices. While he acknowledges that close reading is often the default method of teaching reading within college English courses, he contends that this approach to teaching reading is problematic because students often assimilate texts into their own experiences, thereby making the text mean what they *expect* it to mean so they can relate. As such, Scholes calls for "distant reading" (166) that would compel students to recognize and make sense of difference. He claims that this can be achieved by selecting texts with which students cannot easily and readily identify.

Shanahan, Cynthia, Timothy Shanahan and Cynthia Misischia. 2011. "Analysis of Expert Readers in Three Disciplines: History, Mathematics, and Chemistry." *Journal of Literacy Research* 43.4: 393–429.

The authors describe their findings from a 2011 study that suggest that there are significant consistencies in the ways in which readers—across disciplinary lines—approach disciplinary-specific texts. After using think aloud protocols to analyze the reading habits of professors in chemistry, history, and mathematics, Shanahan and her colleagues found many instances in which they engaged in similar strategies (sourcing, contextualization, corroboration, critiquing of the argument, use of text structure, paying attention to visual or graphical information and chemical and mathematical equations). This exploratory research suggests that although reading strategies may be used to "varying degrees and in unique ways" across disciplines, there is, in fact, overlap among the strategies used by expert readers in disciplines as varied as history and mathematics.

Smith, Frank. 1994. *Understanding Reading: A Psycholinguistic Analysis of Reading and Learning to Read.* 6th ed. Mahwah, NJ: Lawrence Erlbaum.

In this seminal text on reading, Smith uses the preface in this edition to address reviews and alternative perspectives that have emerged since the book's initial publication in 1971. While Smith does not offer strategies for teaching, he glosses the various theories that emerge from fields such as linguistics, psychology, and physiology that have always informed the study and teaching of reading. It is Smith's contention that in order to understand how to teach reading one must develop a familiarity with research from these fields. His book provides a guide to said research in order to foster in its audience an understanding of "reading as an aspect of thinking and learning."

Tate, Gary. 1993. "A Place for Literature in Freshman Composition." *College English* 55.3: 317–321.

> One half of what has been called the Lindemann-Tate debate, Tate argues that literary texts should be included in the first-year writing course because this "excellent writing" (317) helps students improve as writers. He contends that "we should not deny our students the pleasure and profit of reading literature" (319).

Tetreault, Diane DeVido and Carole Center. 2009. "But I'm Not a Reading Teacher!" *Open Words* 3.1: 45–61.

> Tetrault and DeVido argue that the first-year composition classroom offers an opportunity to teach students the practices associated with close, critical reading, and may, in fact, be "one of the last opportunities to reach these students" (45). They describe a range of activities, assignments, and reading materials that have the potential to "deepen" and "broaden" (52) students' reading so that students have the opportunity to rethink and revise their readings and also increase in the amount and variety of reading they complete.

Thelin, William H. 2009. "The Peculiar Relationship to Reading in College Curriculum." *Open Words* 3.1: 1–4.

> In this introduction to the issue, Thelin argues that those in English studies would benefit from "strengthen[ing] our relationship with ideas drawn from K–12 educators and educational theorists" (3). Understanding what is already known about how students read and what motivates them to do so can help post-secondary instructors develop sound reading pedagogies. Collaborations between K–12 and post-secondary instructors, contends Thelin, have the potential to make "reading theory and research an integral part of the curriculum in English studies" (3).

Tompkins, Jane, ed. 1980. *Reader Response Criticism: From Formalism to Post-structuralism.* Baltimore: Johns Hopkins University Press.

> As its subtitle suggests, this anthology traces the development of reader-response criticism from New Criticism through its presence in post-structuralist theory. Key figures whose works are collected include, among others, Walker Gibson, Jonathan Culler, Georges Poulet, Wolfgang Iser, Stanley Fish, David Bleich, and Walter Benn Michaels. The anthology also includes an introductory and final chapter written by Tompkins, as well as an annotated bibliography of reader-oriented work.

Walker, Nancy. 1993. "The Student Reader as Writer." *ADE Bulletin* 106: 35–37.

> Walker argues that helping students read texts in order to notice the decisions the author makes is useful because "the work ceases to be a mere artifact, a stone tablet, and becomes instead a living utterance with immediacy and texture" (36). In emphasizing the published writers' decisions, students are prompted to consider their own writerly choices and the potential effects and implications of them.

APPENDIX B
Handouts from Professional Development Workshops on Integrating Attention to Reading into Courses across the Curriculum

INTEGRATING ATTENTION TO READING IN YOUR COURSES

1. Discuss with students *why* and *how* scholars in your field read.

2. Discuss with students why you assign reading and address its connection to other aspects of the course. Develop assignments that make these connections evident.

3. Talk to students about the range of ways they might read the texts you assign. Address the differences among reading to summarize, paraphrase, and analyze (and any other key terms/methods in your field). Address how these different reading practices lead to the production of different types of texts, and develop assignments that allow students to experience and reflect on these differences.

4. Take the time to name *and define* the reading approach(es) (e.g., rhetorical reading, close reading) you would like students to employ and encourage students to use these names/terms when discussing their reading processes.

5. Talk to students about what they know about themselves as readers. Do they have a default reading approach they take? Do they tend to read for information or other aspects of the text? To what extent do they read print and online texts differently? How does this compare to how you expect them to read? Should they be reading in order to comprehend; to discern how sources are used; to notice the style of writing; to recognize the structure or organization of the piece? All of the above?

6. Show students what it looks like to actively read, including how one annotates a text. Perhaps you can show them what you do or maybe you have a student sample. Students are leery of this

DOI: 10.7330/9780874219609.c009

because they often want to sell books back, but if they annotate in pencil they can erase the markings. Most students use
highlighting, which does not indicate anything about the highlighted text except that it is *important* (and, too often, almost
everything gets highlighted). Show students samples that are
annotated with actual commentary, including questions and
notes in the margins. If they still want to use a highlighter then
make sure they indicate to themselves *what* is important about
each moment in the text.

7. Indicate the resources to which students who are con-
    fused about a text (because of content, style, or any other
    feature) might turn. Can they come to you to ask ques-
    tions? Will the librarians be able to help? A tutor in the
    writing center? Is there a place where they can look up
    difficult ideas/concepts or jargon that are specific to your
    discipline?

ASSIGNMENTS THAT FOREGROUND
READING-WRITING CONNECTIONS

1. Students keep a reading journal/notebook in which they
    document on a regular basis the texts they are reading, their
    responses to the reading, connections they draw among
    readings, and questions they have about the reading. This is
    also a space in which they can track their reading practices,
    including various approaches (e.g., close reading, skimming,
    annotating) they took to the reading, which moments in the
    reading proved challenging, and which reading strategies they
    employed to work through this difficulty.

2. Students read a text in order to ultimately extend or "forward"
    the writer's argument or project. This means that students
    must first take the time to understand the writer's position,
    point of view, and other elements of the text in order to devel-
    op an informed "extension."

3. Teach students how to annotate a text. This might include ask-
    ing students to develop their own marks and a key to them or
    you can specify the elements in each text students are expect-
    ed to notice and mark. You may also encourage students to

develop a "conversation" in the text's margins with the author, through a series of questions, queries, and comments.

4. Ask students to engage with a single text in a range of ways (e.g., close reading, skimming) that you prescribe depending on your goals and reflect on these experiences.

5. Ask students to engage with a single text by applying ways of reading *they* generate either as a class or individuals and reflect on the uses of these approaches within your class and other contexts.

APPENDIX C

Supporting Materials from National Survey of First-Year Composition Instructors and Their Students

ONLINE INSTRUCTOR SURVEY AND ANALYSIS

Below is a snapshot of what first-year instructors saw when they accessed the online survey.

1. Including this year, how long have you been teaching first-year composition?
   - ❏ Less than 1 year
   - ❏ 1–2 years
   - ❏ 3–5 years
   - ❏ 6–10 years
   - ❏ More than 10 years

2. At which type of institution(s) do you teach (check all that apply)?
   - ❏ Four-year college
   - ❏ Four-year university
   - ❏ Two-year institution
   - ❏ Community college
   - ❏ Other

3. How many writing courses, in general, have you taught?
   - ❏ 1–2
   - ❏ 3–5
   - ❏ 6–10
   - ❏ More than 10 courses

4. What is your highest educational background?
   - ❏ PhD
   - ❏ Master's Degree
   - ❏ Bachelor's Degree

5. Your highest degree is in which field?

DOI: 10.7330/9780874219609.c010

6. Which of the following forms of training have you had? (check all that apply)
   - ❏ Completed graduate work in rhetoric and composition
   - ❏ Attended conferences and/or workshops on the teaching of writing
   - ❏ Read articles on teaching writing
   - ❏ Other

7. If you answered "other" to question 6, please explain. Otherwise, continue to next question.

8. Did your training address the role of reading in writing instruction? Explain.

9. Please list those factors that influence how you teach writing (e.g., training, experience, textbooks, mentors, particular theories).

10. How do you define college-level reading?

11. Do students at your institution come prepared to read at the college level?

12. Does your first-year writing course syllabus say anything about reading? If yes, describe.

13. Do you give students any assignments that are reading-focused? If so, please describe.

14. Do you ask students to take different reading approaches to different kinds of texts?
    - ❏ Yes
    - ❏ No

15. What reading skill or kind of reading do you think is most beneficial for your students to learn?

16. Do you think that reading and writing are connected practices?
    - ❏ Yes
    - ❏ No

17. If you answered "yes" just above, how do you highlight or teach these connections in first-year writing?

18. What resources do you consult and/or use in your teaching (e.g. textbooks, handbooks)?

19. What about these resources do you find most beneficial?

20. Would you be interested in taking part in a 15–30 minute follow-up interview? If yes, please provide your email address. You will be compensated for your time.

21. Would you be willing to share a survey link with your students so they can reflect on how they perceive the relationship between reading and writing? Students will not be compensated for completing the survey, but if they agree to a follow-up interview they will be compensated. Please include your email address in the space below and the link will be sent to you so you can share it with your students.

COMMENTARY ABOUT SURVEYS

Although Lauer and Asher (1988, 65) point out that "multiple choice questions are succinct, parsimonious, easily aggregated for analysis, and standardized," the open-ended questions included in the survey are necessary in order to capture the terminology that instructors use to talk about reading and to get a sense of how they articulate and describe the role reading plays in their composition classrooms. Giving respondents the opportunity to choose their own terms for describing reading is especially important because the surveys and interviews are intended to supplement the discussion of professional discourse and the terminology in Chapter 4. In other words, these open-ended questions provide access to the terms and ideas that circulate among instructors of first-year composition, which are not necessarily represented in the field's journals.

In order to analyze my qualitative data, I used coding and microanalyses to organize and focus more intently on particular responses. Both instructor and student audio-recorded interviews were transcribed and then coded thematically, based on the prevalence of recurring themes relevant to my study. The themes generated by the interviews were compared to the survey results in order to determine the prevalence of those themes within the data collected in the surveys. Portions of the surveys and interviews that seemed especially relevant to my study were subject to microanalyses to help "break open the data and to consider all the possible meanings" (Strauss and Corbin 1998, 59). In order to triangulate the data, interviews of participants were read against their individual surveys in order to compare their responses, as well as validate my interpretations of them. In accordance with my University's IRB policies, all survey data was collected anonymously. All participants were informed of the purpose of the research, their right to refuse to answer any question, and the goals of the study. All interviewees were assigned a pseudonym, which are used to report and analyze the data.

INSTRUCTOR PHONE INTERVIEW GUIDE

1. Can you describe the kinds of reading that students are expected to do in your first-year writing course?

2. Do these expectations change depending on the particular students or the school at which you are teaching?

3. How is this reading incorporated—if at all—into assignments for the course?

4. How do you imagine this reading is connected to the writing for the course?

5. Do you address these connections with students? If so, how?

6. What materials support this pedagogy in your classrooms?

7. Is there anything else you would like to share about the course?

STUDENT PHONE INTERVIEW GUIDE

1. Please describe the kind of reading you did in your first-year writing course.

2. Please describe the kind of writing you did in this course.

3. As a student in the course were you encouraged to recognize or explore connections between reading and writing for the course? If so, in what ways?

4. What purpose did reading for the course seem to serve?

5. Did different texts seem to serve different purposes?

6. To what extent (if at all) did your instructor talk about reading? Explain.

7. Where you taught different reading approaches or strategies? If yes, please describe these.

8. What motivated you (if anything) to read for the course?

9. How was reading important (if at all) to out of class assignments and in-class exercises?

10. How would you describe your level of engagement as you read for the course?

11. Is there anything else you would like to share about the course?

ONLINE STUDENT SURVEY

1. Are you 18 years of age or older? Please note that if you are not 18 you cannot take this survey.
   - ❏ Yes
   - ❏ No

2. What is the name of the writing instructor who gave you the link to this survey? Remember that your instructor does not have access to your answers.

3. Which type of institution do you attend?
   - ❏ Four-year college
   - ❏ Four-year university
   - ❏ Two-year institution
   - ❏ Community College

4. How did you choose to enroll in your first-year writing course? (Choose all that apply)
   - ❏ Chose whatever course was open
   - ❏ Chose based on the instructor
   - ❏ Chose a topic I liked
   - ❏ Other

5. If you chose "Other" for the previous question, describe your reasoning for choosing the course.

6. What did you expect from your first-year writing course?

7. Describe your overall experience in your first-year writing course.

8. Describe how your first-year writing course compares to a high school writing or English course.

9. How would you compare the types of texts you read in your first-year writing class to those you read on your own outside of the class?

10. Do you find that the reading you do for your first-year writing course helps you as a writer? Answer yes or no and explain your answer.

11. How would you describe the type of reading your first-year writing instructor expects?

12. Do you feel motivated to read for your first-year writing course?
   ❏ Yes
   ❏ No

13. Have you learned about or experienced any connections between reading and writing in this course? Explain.

14. Would you be interested in participating in a 15-minute follow-up phone interview? Please answer yes or no. *If yes, please include your email address. You will be paid $10 for your time.*

REFERENCES

Adler-Kassner, Linda, and Heidi Estrem. 2007. "Reading Practices in the Writing Classroom." *WPA* 31.1–2: 35–47.

Allen, Ira James. 2012. "Reprivileging Reading: The Negotiation of Uncertainty." *Pedagogy* 12 (1): 97–120. http://dx.doi.org/10.1215/15314200-1416540.

Anderson, Daniel, Anthony Atkins, Cheryl Ball, Krista Homicz Millar, Cynthia Selfe, and Richard Selfe. 2006. "Integrating Multimodality into Composition Curricula: Survey Methodology and Results from a CCCC Research Initiative Grant." *Compositions Studies* 34 (2): 59–84.

Applebee, Arthur N. 1974. *Tradition and Reform in the Teaching of English.* Illinois: NCTE.

Atkins, G. Douglas, and Michael L. Johnson, eds. 1985. *Writing and Reading Differently.* Lawrence: University Press of Kansas.

Audrey [pseud]. 2012. Interview by Ellen Carillo. 23 March.

Bailey [pseud]. 2012. Interview by Ellen Carillo. 15 March.

Baker, William D. 1953. "Teach Us to Read." *College English* 14 (4): 232–4. http://dx.doi.org/10.2307/372575.

Barbara [pseud]. 2012. Interview by Ellen Carillo. 27 April.

Bartholomae, David. 1996. "The Argument of Reading." In *Writing on the Margins: Essays on Composition and Teaching*, ed. David Bartholomae, 244–54. New York: Bedford/St. Martin's.

Bartholomae, David. 2005. "Reading and Writing in the Academy." In *Writing on the Margins: Essays on Composition and Teaching*, ed. David Bartholomae, 358–71. New York: Bedford/St. Martin's.

Bartholomae, David. 2007. "Writing with Texts: An Interview with David Bartholomae." *The Minnesota Review*, 95–115.

Bartholomae, David. 2011. Interview by Ellen Carillo. 29 July.

Bartholomae, David, and Anthony R. Petrosky. 1986. "A Basic Reading and Writing Course for the College Curriculum." In *Facts, Artifacts, and Counterfacts*, ed. David Bartholomae and Anthony Petrosky, 3–43. Portsmouth, NH: Boynton/Cook.

Bartholomae, David, and Anthony R. Petrosky, eds. 1987. *Ways of Reading.* 1st ed. New York: Bedford/St. Martin's.

Bartholomae, David, Anthony R. Petrosky, and Stacey Waite. 2014. *Ways of Reading.* 10th ed. New York: Bedford/St. Martin's.

Bartholomae, David, and Beth Matway. 2010. "The Pittsburgh Study of Writing." *Across the Disciplines.* http://wac.colostate.edu/atd/articles/bartholomae_matway2010/index.cfm.

Bawarshi, Anis. 2003. *Genre and the Invention of the Writer.* Logan: Utah State University Press.

Barawshi, Anis, and Mary Jo Reiff. 2004. *Genre: An Introduction to History, Theory, Research and Pedagogy.* West Lafayette, IN: Parlor Press.

Bazerman, Charles. 1980. "A Relationship between Reading and Writing: The Conversation Model." *College Composition and Communication* 41 (6): 656–61.

DOI: 10.7330/9780874219609.c011

Bazerman, Charles. 2009. "Genre and Cognitive Development: Beyond Writing to Learn." In *Genre in a Changing World*, ed. Charles Bazerman, Adair Bonini, and Débora de Carvalho Figueiredo 279–94. West Lafayette, IN: WAC Clearinghouse/Parlor Press; http://education.ucsb.edu/bazerman/chapters/documents/Bazerman2009ChptrGenreandCognit.pdf.

Beach, King. 1999. "Consequential Transitions: A Sociocultural Expedition beyond Transfer in Education." *Review of Research in Education* 24:101–39.

Beaufort, Anne. 2007. *College Writing and Beyond*. Logan. Utah State University Press.

Benander, Ruth, and Robin Lightner. 2005. "Promoting Transfer of Learning: Connecting General Education Courses." *Journal of General Education* 54 (3): 199–208. http://dx.doi.org/10.1353/jge.2006.0001.

Bereiter, Carl. 1995. "A Dispositional View of Transfer." In *Teaching for Transfer*, ed. Anne McKeough, Judy Lupart, and Anthony Marini, 21–34. Mahwah, NJ: Lawrence Erlbaum.

Berthoff, Ann E. 1981a. *Forming/Thinking/Writing*. Montclair, NJ: Boynton/Cook.

Berthoff, Ann E. 1981b. *The Making of Meaning: Metaphors, Models, and Maxims for Writing Teachers*. Montclair, NJ: Boynton/Cook.

Berthoff, Ann E. 1982. "How We Construe Is How We Construct." Comppile. org. 84–86.

Bizzell, Patricia. 1986. "On the Possibility of a Unified Theory of Composition and Literature." *Rhetoric Review* 4 (2): 174–80. http://dx.doi.org/10.1080/07350198609359121.

Blau, Sheridan. 2003. *The Literature Workshop*. Portsmouth, NH: Heinemann.

Booth, Wayne. 1956. "Imaginative Literature is Indispensable." *College Composition and Communication* 7 (1): 35–8. http://dx.doi.org/10.2307/355597.

Booth, Wayne. 1983. "LITCOMP." In *Composition and Literature*, ed. Winifred Bryan Horner, 157–80. Chicago: University of Chicago Press.

Brandt, Deborah. 2011. "A Commentary on 'One Story of Many to Be Told': Following Empirical Studies of Student and Adult Writing through 100 Years of NCTE Journals." *Research in the Teaching of English* 46 (2): 210–4.

Brent, Doug. 1992. *Reading as Rhetorical Invention*. Urbana, IL: NCTE.

Brereton, John C., ed. 1996. *The Origins of Composition in American Colleges: 1875–1925*. Pittsburgh: University of Pittsburgh Press.

Brooks, Cleanth, and Robert Penn Warren. 1950. *Understanding Poetry*. New York: Holt.

Brower, Rueben, and Richard A. Poirer, eds. 1962. *In Defense of Reading: A Reader's Approach to Literary Criticism*. Boston: E. P. Dutton.

Bunn, Michael Thomson. 2010. "Reconceptualizing the Role of Reading in Composition Studies." Diss., University of Michigan. http://deepblue.lib.umich.edu/handle/2027.42/77796.

Bunn, Mike. 2011. "How to Read like a Writer." In *Writing Spaces: Readings on Writing*, vol. 2., ed. Charles Lowe and Pavel Zemliansky, 71–86. Anderson, SC: Parlor Press.

Bunn, Mike. 2013. "Motivation and Connection: Teaching Reading (and Writing) in the Composition Classroom." *College Composition and Communication* 64 (3): 496–516.

Campione, Joseph C., Amy M. Shapiro, and Ann L. Brown. 1995. "Forms of Transfer in a Community of Learners: Flexible Learning and Understanding."

In *Teaching for Transfer*, ed. Anne McKeough, Judy Lupart, and Anthony Marini, 35–68. Mahwah, NJ: Lawrence Erlbaum.

Carr, Jean Ferguson, Stephen L. Carr, and Lucille M. Schultz. 2005. *Archives of Instruction: Nineteenth-Century Rhetorics, Readers, and Composition Books in the United States*. Carbondale: Southern Illinois University Press.

Charney, Davida. 1996. "Empiricism Is not a Four-Letter Word." *College Composition and Communication* 47 (4): 567–93. http://dx.doi.org/10.2307/358602.

Clifford, John, and John Schilb. 1985. "Composition Theory and Literary Theory." In *Perspectives on Research and Scholarship in Composition*, ed. Ben W. McClelland and Timothy R. Donovan, 45–67. New York: MLA.

Comprone, Joseph J. 1983. "Recent Research in Reading and Its Implications for the College Composition Curriculum." *Rhetoric Review* 1 (2): 122–37. http://dx.doi.org/10.1080/07350198309359044.

Connors, Robert J. 1997. *Composition-Rhetoric*. Pittsburgh: University of Pittsburgh Press.

Connors, Robert J. 1989. "Rhetorical History as a Component of Composition Studies." *Rhetoric Review* 7 (2): 230–40. http://dx.doi.org/10.1080/0735019 8909388858.

Connors, Robert J. 1986. "Textbooks and the Evolution of the Discipline." *College Composition and Communication* 37 (2): 178–94. http://dx.doi.org/10.2307 /357516.

Comley, Nancy. 1985. "A Release from Weak Specifications: Liberating the Student Reader." In *Writing and Reading Differently*, ed. Douglas Atkins and Michael Johnson, 129–38. Lawrence: University Press of Kansas.

Comley, Nancy R., and Robert Scholes. 1983. "Literature, Composition, and the Structure of English." In *Composition and Literature: Bridging the Gap*, ed. Winifred Bryan Horner, 96–109. Chicago: University of Chicago Press.

Crowley, Sharon. 1998. *Composition in the University*. Pittsburgh: University of Pittsburgh Press.

Daniell, Beth. 2003. *A Communion of Friendship: Literacy, Spiritual Practice and Women in Recovery*. Urbana: Southern Illinois University Press.

Devitt, Amy, Mary Jo Reiff, and Anis Bawarshi. 2004. *Scenes of Writing: Strategies for Composing with Genres*. New York: Longman.

Darla [pseud]. 2012. Interview by Ellen Carillo. 23 March.

Deena. [pseud]. 2012. Interview by Ellen Carillo. 6 March.

Dixon, John. 1975. *Growth through English*. Urbana, IL: NCTE.

Detterman, Douglas K., ed. 1993. "The Case for the Prosecution: Transfer as an Epiphenomenon." In *Transfer on Trial: Intelligence, Cognition, and Instruction*, 1–24. Norwood, NJ: Ablex.

Donahue, Patricia. 2009. "How Well Do Your Students Read?" *WPA-L*, October 27.

Downs, Doug. 2010. "Teaching First-Year Writers to Use Texts: Scholarly Readings in Writing-about-Writing in First-Year Comp." *Reader* 60:19–50.

Duke, Nell K., and David Pearson. 2011. "Essential Elements of Fostering and Teaching Reading Comprehension." In *What Research Has to Say about Reading Instruction*, 4th ed., ed. S. Jay Samuels and Alan E. Farstrup, 51–93. Newark, DE: International Reading Association. http://dx.doi.org/10.1598 /0829.03.

Eagleton, Terry. 1983. *Literary Theory: An Introduction*. Minneapolis: University of Minnesota Press.

Eblen, Charlene. 1983. "Writing across the Curriculum: A Survey of University Faculty Views and Classroom Practices." *Research in the Teaching of English* 17 (4): 333–48.

Edmundson, Mark. 2009. "Against Readings." *Profession* 2009 (1): 56–65. http://dx.doi.org/10.1632/prof.2009.2009.1.56.

Elbow, Peter. 1993. "The War between Reading and Writing—and How to End It." *Rhetoric Review* 12 (1): 5–24. http://dx.doi.org/10.1080/0735019 9309389024.

Erma [pseud]. 2012. Interview by Ellen Carillo. 15 March.

Farah [pseud]. 2012. Interview by Ellen Carillo. 13 March.

Farmer, Frank M., and Phillip K. Arrington. 1993. "Apologies and Accommodations: Imitation and the Writing Process." *Rhetoric Society Quarterly* 23 (1): 12–34. http://dx.doi.org/10.1080/02773949309390976.

Fleckenstein, Kristie. 2003. *Embodied Literacies: Imageword and a Poetics of Teaching*. Urbana: Southern Illinois University Press.

Flesch, Rudolf. 1955. *Why Johnny Can't Read—and What You Can Do about It*. New York: William Morrow.

Flower, Linda. 1988. "The Construction of Purpose in Writing and Reading." *College English* 50 (5): 528–50. http://dx.doi.org/10.2307/377490.

Flynn, Elizabeth. 1982. "Peer Tutoring and Reading Activities." Conference on College Composition and Communication. Lecture.

Foertsch, Julie. 1995. "Where Cognitive Psychology Applies: How Theories about Memory and Transfer Can Influence Composition Pedagogy." *Written Communication* 12 (3): 360–83. http://dx.doi.org/10.1177/0741088395012 003006.

Fulwiler, Toby, and Art Young. 1982. *Language Connections: Writing and Reading across the Curriculum*. Urbana, IL: NCTE.

Gena [pseud]. 2012. Interview by Ellen Carillo. 13 March.

Golding, Alan. 1995. *From Outlaw to Classic*. Madison: University of Wisconsin Press.

Goodman, Kenneth. 1996. *On Reading*. Portsmouth, NH: Heinemann.

Graff, Gerald. 2009. "Introduction." *Profession* 2009 (1): 5–10. http://dx.doi.org /10.1632/prof.2009.2009.1.5.

Graff, Gerald. 2007. *Professing Literature*. Chicago: University of Chicago Press. http://dx.doi.org/10.7208/chicago/9780226305257.001.0001.

Graff, Gerald, and Cathy Birkenstein. 2009. *They Say/I Say: The Moves that Matter in Academic Writing*. 2nd ed. New York: Norton.

Grey, Lennox. 1943. "Communication and War: An Open Letter to English Teachers." *English Journal* 32 (1): 12–3. http://dx.doi.org/10.2307/805692.

Haas, Christina, and Linda Flower. 1988. "Rhetorical Reading Strategies and the Construction of Meaning." *College Composition and Communication* 39 (2): 167–83. http://dx.doi.org/10.2307/358026.

Harkin, Patricia. 2005. "The Reception of Reader-Response Theory." *College Composition and Communication* 56 (3): 410–25.

Harrington, Dana. 1997. "Composition, Literature, and the Emergence of Modern Reading Practices." *Rhetoric Review* 15 (2): 249–63. http://dx.doi.org /10.1080/07350199709359218.

Harris, Joseph. 2006. *Rewriting: How to Do Things with Texts*. *Logan*. Utah State University Press.

Harris, Joseph. 1997. *A Teaching Subject*. Upper Saddle River, NJ: Prentice Hall.

Hart, John A., Robert C. Stack, and Neal Woodruff, Jr. 1958. "Literature in the Composition Course." *College Composition and Communication* 9 (4): 236–41.

Haskell, Robert E. 2001. *Transfer of Learning: Cognition, Instruction, and Reasoning*. New York: Academic Press.

Haswell, Richard. 2005. "NCTE/CCCC's Recent War on Scholarship." *Written Communication* 22 (2): 198–223. http://dx.doi.org/10.1177/0741088305275367.

Haswell, Richard, T. L. Briggs, J. A. Fay, N. K. Gillen, R. Harrill, A. M. Shupala, and S. S. Trevino. 1999. "Context and Rhetorical Reading Strategies: Haas and Flower (1988) Revisited." *Written Communication* 16 (3): 3–27. http://dx.doi.org/10.1177/0741088399016001001.

Hayford, Harrison. 1956. "Literature in English A at Northwestern." *College Composition and Communication* 7 (1): 42–5. http://dx.doi.org/10.2307/355599.

Helmers, Marguerite, ed. 2002. *Intertexts: Reading Pedagogy in College Writing Classrooms*. Mahwah, NJ: Lawrence Erlbaum Associates.

Henry, Jeanne. 2009. "Cultivating Reading Workshop: New Theory into Practice." Open *Words* 3(1): 62–74.

Horner, Winifred Bryan, ed. 1983. *Composition and Literature: Bridging the Gap*. Chicago: University of Chicago Press.

Horning, Alice S. 1987. "The Trouble with Reading Is the Trouble with Writing." *Journal of Basic Writing* 6 (1): 36–47.

Horning, Alice S. 2007. "Reading across the Curriculum as the Key to Student Success." *Across the Disciplines* 4. http://wac.colostate.edu/atd/articles/horning2007.cfm.

Horning, Alice S. 2013. *Reading, Writing, and Digitizing Literacy in the Electronic Age*. Cambridge: Cambridge Scholars Press.

Horning, Alice S., and Elizabeth Kraemer, eds. 2013. *Reconnecting Reading and Writing*. Anderson, SC: Parlor Press.

Howard, Rebecca Moore, Tricia Serviss, and Tanya K. Rodrigue. 2010. "Writing from Sources, Writing from Sentences." *Writing & Pedagogy* 2 (2): 177–92. http://dx.doi.org/10.1558/wap.v2i2.177.

Hutchinson, E. J. 1955. "The Teaching of Reading in the Freshman Course." *College Composition and Communication* 6 (2): 94–96.

Huffman, Deborah. 2007. "Reading by the Book: An Examination of Reading Pedagogy in Introductory Composition Textbooks." Diss., University of Indiana. Books.google.com.

Huffman, Deborah. 2010. "Towards Modes of Reading in Composition." *Reader* 60:162–88.

Hyland, Terry. 2011. *Mindfulness and Learning*. New York: Springer. http://dx.doi.org/10.1007/978-94-007-1911-8.

Jarna [pseud]. 2012. Interview by Ellen Carillo. 27 March.

Jolliffe, David A. 2007. "Learning to Read as Continuing Education." *College Composition and Communication* 58 (3): 470–94.

Jolliffe, David A. 2003. "Who Is Teaching Composition Students to Read and How Are They Doing It?" *Composition Studies* 31 (1): 127–42.

Jolliffe, David A., and Allison Harl. 2008. "Studying the 'Reading Transition' from High School to College: What Are Our Students Reading and Why?" *College English* 70 (6): 599–617.

Julia [pseud]. 2012. Interview by Ellen Carillo. 29 March.

Kaila [pseud]. 2012. Interview by Ellen Carillo. 24 April.

Katie [pseud]. 2012. Interview by Ellen Carillo. 27 March.

Keller, Daniel. 2013. *Chasing Literacy: Reading and Writing in an Age of Acceleration.* Logan: Utah State University Press.

Kitzhaber, Albert. 1963. *Themes, Theories, and Therapy.* New York: McGraw Hill.

Kitzhaber, Albert. 1966. "What Is English?" *Working Papers of the Anglo-American Seminar on the Teaching and Learning of English.* Dartmouth, NH. ED082201.

Langer, Ellen. 2000. "Mindful Learning." *Current Directions in Psychological Science* 9 (6): 220–3. http://dx.doi.org/10.1111/1467-8721.00099.

Lauer, Janice M., and J. William Asher. 1988. *Composition Research/Empirical Designs.* New York: Oxford.

Leu, Donald J., Charles K. Kinzer, Julie L. Coiro, Dana W. Cammack. 2004. "Toward a Theory of New Literacies Emerging from the Internet and Other Information and Communication Technologies." In *Theoretical Models and Processes of Reading*, ed. Robert B. Ruddell and Norman J. Unrau, 1570–613. Newark, DE: International Reading Association.

Lindemann, Erika. 1993. "Freshman Composition: No Place for Literature." *College English* 55 (3): 311–6. http://dx.doi.org/10.2307/378743.

Lunsford, Andrea A., John J. Ruszkiewicz, and Keith Walters, eds. 2010. "Preface." In *Everything's an Argument: With Readings*, 5th ed., v–xiv. Boston: Bedford St. Martin's.

Lynda [pseud]. 2012. Interview by Ellen Carillo. 14 March.

Marla [pseud]. 2012. Interview by Ellen Carillo. 30 March.

Marshall [pseud]. 2012. Interview by Ellen Carillo. 6 March.

Mayer, Richard E., and Merlin C. Wittrock. 1996. "Problem-Solving Transfer." In *Handbook of Educational Psychology*, ed. David C. Berliner and Robert C. Calfee, 47–62. New York: Macmillan Library Reference.

McCormick, Kathleen. 1994. *The Culture of Reading / The Teaching of English.* Manchester: Manchester University Press.

Miller, Susan, ed. 2009. *The Norton Book of Composition Studies.* New York: Norton.

Morrow, Nancy. 1997. "The Role of Reading in the Composition Classroom." *JAC* 17 (3): 453–72.

Muller, Herbert. 1967. *The Uses of English.* New York: Holt.

Murphy, James. 1982. "Rhetorical History as a Guide to Salvation of American Reading and Writing: A Plea for Curricular Courage." In *The Rhetorical Tradition and Modern Writing*, ed. James Murphy, 3–12. New York: MLA.

Murray, Donald M. 1982. "Teaching the Other Self: The Writer's First Reader." *College Composition and Communication* 33 (2): 140–7.

Myers, Miles. 1996. *Changing Our Minds: Negotiating English and Literacy.* Urbana, IL: NCTE.

Nelms, Gerald, and Rhonda Leathers Dively. 2007. "Perceived Roadblocks to Transferring Knowledge from First-Year Composition to Writing-Intensive Major Courses: A Pilot Study." *WPA* 31.1–2: 214–240.

Nelson, Nancy. 1998. "Reading and Writing Contextualized." In *The Reading-Writing Connection*, edited by Nancy Nelson and Robert C. Calfee, 266–85. Chicago: University of Chicago Press.

Newkirk, Thomas, ed. 1986. *Only Connect: Uniting Reading and Writing.* Montclair, NJ: Boynton/Cook.

North, Stephen. 1987. *The Making of Knowledge in Composition.* Upper Montclair, NJ: Boynton.

Nystrand, Martin, Stuart Greene, and Jeffrey Wiemelt. 1993. "Where Did Composition Studies Come from?" *Written Communication* 31 (2): 267–333.

Ong, Walter J. 1960. "Wired for Sound: Teaching, Communications, and Technological Culture." *College English* 21 (5): 245–51.

Palinscar, Annmarie Sullivan, and Ann L. Brown. 1984. "Reciprocal Teaching of Comprehension-Fostering and Comprehension-Monitoring Activities." *Cognition and Instruction* 1 (2): 117–75. http://dx.doi.org/10.1207/s1532690xci0102_1.

Paxman, David. 1984. "Reinventing the Composition/Literature Course." *Rhetoric Review* 2 (2): 124–32. http://dx.doi.org/10.1080/07350198409359065.

Penrose, Ann M., and Barbara Sitko, eds. 1993. *Hearing Ourselves Think: Cognitive Research in the College Writing Classroom.* New York: Oxford University Press.

Perkins, David, and Gavriel Salomon. 1988. "Teaching for Transfer." *Educational Leadership* 46 (1): 22–32. http://www.ascd.org/ASCD/pdf/journals/ed_lead/el_198809_perkins.pdf.

Perkins, David, and Gavriel Salomon. 1992. "Transfer of Learning." In *International Encyclopedia of Education*, 2nd ed. Oxford: Pergamon Press. http://learnweb.harvard.edu/alps/thinking/docs/traencyn.html.

Perkins, David, and Gavriel Salomon. 1989. "Are Cognitive Skills Context Bound?" *Educational Researcher* 18 (1): 16–25. http://dx.doi.org/10.3102/0013189X018001016.

Petersen, Bruce T., ed. 1986. *Convergences: Transactions in Reading and Writing.* Urbana, IL: NCTE.

Petrosky, Anthony. 1982. "From Story to Essay: From Reading to Writing." *College Composition and Communication* 33 (1): 19–37. http://dx.doi.org/10.2307/357842.

Phelps, William Lyon. 1912. *Teaching in School and College.* New York: Macmillian.

Phelps, Louise Wetherbee. 1986. "The Domain of Composition." *Rhetoric Review* 4 (2): 182–95. http://dx.doi.org/10.1080/07350198609359122.

Pressley, Michael. 1990. *Cognitive Strategy Instruction that Really Improves Children's Academic Performance.* Cambridge, MA: Brookline.

Purves, Alan C. 1983. "'Language Processing: Reading and Writing.' Rev. of *Language Processing and the Reading of Literature: Toward a Model of Comprehension and Constructing Texts; Elements of a Theory of Composition and Style*, by George Dillon." *College English* 45 (2): 129–40. http://dx.doi.org/10.2307/377220.

Qualley, Donna. 1997. *Turns of Thought.* Portsmouth, NH: Boynton/Cook.

Raina [pseud]. 2012. Interview by Ellen Carillo. March 27.

Richards, I. A. 1929. *Practical Criticism.* London: Routlege.

"Robert Penn Warren, Poet and Author, Dies." 1989. Obituary. *New York Times.* 16 Sept. http://topics.nytimes.com/top/reference/timestopics/people/w/robert_penn_warren/index.html.

Raub, Albert N. 1882. *Studies in English and American Literature*. Philadelphia: Baub & Co.

Rosenwasser, David, and Jill Stephen. 2011. *Writing Analytically*. 6th ed. Boston: Wadsworth.

Russell, David. 1995. "Activity Theory and Its Implications for Writing Instruction." In *Reconceiving Writing, Rethinking Writing Instruction*, ed. Joseph Petraglia, 51–78. Hillsdale, NJ: Erlbaum.

Salvatori, Mariolina Rizzi. 1983. "Reading and Writing a Text: Correlations between Reading and Writing Patterns." *College English* 45 (7): 657–66. http://dx.doi.org/10.2307/377175.

Salvatori, Mariolina Rizzi. 1996a. "'The Argument of Reading' in the Teaching of Composition." In *Argument Revisited; Argument Redefined*, ed. Barbara Emmel, Paula Resch, and Deborah Tenney, 181–97. Thousand Oaks, CA: Sage.

Salvatori, Mariolina Rizzi. 1996b. "Conversations with Texts: Reading in the Teaching of Composition." *College English* 58 (4): 440–54. http://dx.doi.org/10.2307/378854.

Salvatori, Mariolina Rizzi, and Patricia Donahue. 2005. *The Elements (and Pleasures) of Difficulty*. New York: Longman.

Salvatori, Mariolina Rizzi, and Patricia Donahue. 2012. "Stories about Reading: Appearance, Disappearance, Morphing, and Revival." *College English* 75 (2): 199–217.

Scholes, Robert. 1999. *The Rise and Fall of English*. New Haven, CT: Yale University Press.

Scholes, Robert. 2002. "The Transition to College Reading." *Pedagogy* 2 (2): 165–72. http://dx.doi.org/10.1215/15314200-2-2-165.

Schultz, Lucille M. 1999. *The Young Composers: Composition's Beginnings in Nineteenth-Century Schools*. Carbondale: Southern Illinois University Press.

Schwegler, Bob. 2009. "How Well Do Your Students Read?" *WPA-L*, October 27.

Shanahan, Cynthia, Timothy Shanahan, and Cynthia Misischia. 2011. "Analysis of Expert Readers in Three Disciplines: History, Mathematics, and Chemistry." *Journal of Literacy Research* 43 (4): 393–429. http://dx.doi.org/10.1177/1086296X11424071.

Shapiro, Shauna. 2009. "The Integration of Mindfulness and Psychology." *Journal of Clinical Psychology* 65 (6): 555–60. http://dx.doi.org/10.1002/jclp.20602.

Sheryl [pseud]. 2012. Interview by Ellen Carillo. April 24.

Skinnell, Ryan. 2009. "How Well Do Your Students Read?" *WPA-L*, October 27.

Smit, David. 2004. *The End of Composition Studies*. Carbondale: Southern Illinois University Press.

Smith, Frank. 1994. *Understanding Reading: A Psycholinguistic Analysis of Reading and Learning to Read*. 6th ed. Mahwah, NJ: Lawrence Erlbaum.

Smith, Louise A. 1988. *Audits of Meaning*. New York: Heinemann.

Squire, James R. 1983. "Composing and Comprehending: Two Sides of the Same Basic Process." *Language Arts* 60: 581–89.

Steiner, David. 2009. "Reading." *Profession* 2009 (1): 50–5. http://dx.doi.org/10.1632/prof.2009.2009.1.50.

Strauss, Anselm, and Juliet M. Corbin. 1998. *Basics of Qualitative Research*. 2nd ed. New York: Sage.

Swinton, William. 1880. *Studies in English Literature*. New York: Harper & Brothers.

Taczak, Kara. 2012. "The Question of Transfer." *Composition Forum* 26. http://compositionforum.com/issue/26/.

Tate, Gary. 1993. "A Place for Literature in Freshman Composition." *College English* 55 (3): 317–21. http://dx.doi.org/10.2307/378744.

Thaiss, Chris, and Terry Myers Zawacki. 2006. *Engaged Writers and Dynamic Disciplines: Research on the Academic Writing Life*. New York: Heinemann.

Thelin, William H. 2009a. "The Peculiar Relationship to Reading in College Curriculum." *Open Words* 3 (1): 1–4.

Thelin, William H. 2009b. "How Well Do Your Students Read?" *WPA-L*, October 27.

Thorson, Gerald. 1953. "Literature in Freshman English." *College Composition and Communication* 4 (2): 38–40. http://dx.doi.org/10.2307/354041.

Tim [pseud]. 2012. Interview by Ellen Carillo. 24 March.

Thorson, Gerald. 1956. "Literature: The Freshman's Key." *College Composition and Communication* 7 (1): 38–42. http://dx.doi.org/10.2307/355598.

Tierney, Robert J., Patricia L. Anders, and Judy Nichols Mitchell, eds. 1987. *Understanding Readers' Understanding: Theory and Practice*. New York: Routledge.

Trimbur, John. 1994. "*Review: Taking the Social Turn: Teaching Writing Post-Process.*" *College Composition and Communication* 45 (1): 108–18. http://dx.doi.org/10.2307/358592.

Trimbur, John, and Diana George. 1999. "The 'Communication Battle' Or Whatever Happened to the Fourth 'C'?" *College Composition and Communication* 50 (4): 682–98.

Vande Kopple, William J. 1982. "Functional Sentence Perspective, Composition, and Reading." *College Composition and Communication* 33 (1): 5–63.

Villanueva, Victor, and Kristin L. Arola. 2011. *Cross-Talk in Comp Theory: A Reader*. 3rd ed. Urbana, IL: NCTE.

Wanda [pseud]. 2012. Interview by Ellen Carillo. 24 April.

Wardle, Elizabeth. 2007. "Understanding 'Transfer' from FYC: Preliminary Results of a Longitudinal Study." *WPA* 31.1–2: 65–85.

Wardle, Elizabeth. 2009. "'Mutt Genres' and the Goal of FYC: Can We Help Students Write the Genres of the University?" *College Composition and Communication* 60:765–89.

Wardle, Elizabeth, and Doug Downs. 2010. *Writing about Writing: A College Reader*. Boston: Bedford/St. Martin's.

Wells, Jennifer. 2009. "How Well Do Your Students Read?" *WPA-L*, October 27.

"WPA Outcomes Statement for First-Year Composition." 2008. Council of Writing Program Administrators. http://wpacouncil.org/positions/outcomes.html.

Yancey, Kathleen Blake. 2004. "Made Not Only in Words: Composition in a New Key." Chairs address, Conference on College Composition and Communication, San Antonio, Texas, March 25.

ABOUT THE AUTHOR

ELLEN C. CARILLO is Assistant Professor of English at the University of Connecticut and the Writing Program Coordinator at its Waterbury Campus. She teaches undergraduate and graduate courses in composition and literature, and her scholarship has been published in *Rhetoric Review*, *The Writing Lab Newsletter*, *Reader: Essays in Reader-Oriented Theory, Criticism, and Pedagogy*; *Feminist Teacher*, and *Currents in Teaching and Learning*.

INDEX

close reading, 1, 17, 19, 30, 45, 54–55, 94, 110, 113–14, 117, 119–21, 124, 132, 134–36

College Writing and Beyond (Beaufort), 109

Comley, Nancy, 71, 83, 89; "Literature, Composition, and the Structure of English," 90

communication(s), 17, 55, 57, 58, 60, 64, 77, 151; courses and programs, 36, 56, 60, 63; as literature, 58; 60; "postwar movement," 55–57

Composition and Literature: Bridging the Gap (Horner), 77–78, 87, 162

Composition Forum, "Writing and Transfer," 109–10

"Composition Theory and Literary Theory" (Clifford and Schilb), 83–85

Comprone, Joseph, 168; "Recent Research in Reading and Its Implications for the College Composition Classroom," 75

Conference on College Composition and Communication (CCCC), 6, 7, 12, 14–17, 22, 45, 56, 59–60, 63, 81, 85, 118, 143, 145, 149–52; "Reading in the First-Year Writing Classroom," 16, 22, 25; "Writing Assessment Principles Statement," 150

Connors, Robert, 46–47, 49–50, 55, 63, 79–80

"Context and Rhetorical Reading Strategies: Haas and Flower (1988) Revisited" (Haas and Flower), 34, 161

Convergences: Transactions of Reading and Writing (Petersen), 74, 168

"Conversations with Texts: Reading in the Teaching of Composition" (Salvatori), 83, 170

critical reading, 12, 19, 30, 43n6, 54, 59, 97–98, 110, 117, 120, 151, 164, 172

Cross-Talk in Comp Theory: A Reader, (Villanueva and Arola), 2, 21, 76, 146

Crowley, Sharon, 13, 56, 71, 86

Dartmouth seminar, 17, 45, 60, 65–72

de Man, Paul, *Allegories of Reading*, 55

Detterman, Douglas K., *Transfer on Trial*, 116n1

Devitt, Amy, *Scenes of Writing*, 112, 116n4

difficult: in teaching, 34, 65, 122, 133, 150, 158, 174; texts, 61, 67, 70–71, 73n4, 98, 99, 133, 140, 155; transfer, 106. *See also* difficulty; difficulty paper

difficulty: in reading, 125, 127; in teaching, 34, 41; of texts, 70–71; as a tool, 61, 67, 70, 88, 99, 140, 170. *See also* difficult; difficulty paper

difficulty paper, 87, 95, 107, 130. *See also* difficult; difficulty

"Dispositional View of Transfer, A" (Bereiter), 115

Dively, Rhonda Leathers, "Perceived Roadblocks to Transferring Knowledge from First-Year Composition to Writing-Intensive Major Courses," 109–10

Dixon, John, *Growth through English*, 69

Donahue, Patricia, 5, 67, 95, 135; *The Elements (and Pleasures) of Difficulty*, 70, 71, 88, 140; "How Well Do Your Students Read?" 2; *Reader*, 101n1; "Stories about Reading," 4, 6, 7, 93, 143

Downs, Doug: "Teaching First-Year Writers to Use Texts," 141n3, 159; *Writing about Writing*, 119–20

Eagleton, Terry, 55, 83

Eblen, Charlene, 29, 37

"Eclectic Readers," McGuffey Series (McGuffey), 48

Elbow, Peter, "The War Between Reading and Writing—and How to End It," 20n3, 159

Elements (and Pleasures) of Difficulty, The (Salvatori and Donahue), 70, 71, 88, 140

Embodied Literacies (Fleckenstein), 141n2

Emig, Janet, 71